WOK

COOKBOOK FOR BEGINNERS

Wok Cookbook For Beginners: Master the Basics of Wok Cooking and Easily Create Authentic Home-Style and Restaurant-Style Dishes | Includes Expert Techniques & Insider Tips for Perfect Wok Recipes

Emily Rivers

Table of Content

INTRODUCTION

Welcome to "Wok Cookbook for Beginners," your go-to resource for learning the art of wok cooking. Imagine this: it's a cozy evening at home, and instead of picking up the phone to place a takeaway order, you grab your wok. The sounds of sizzling food and the enticing smells of freshly chopped ingredients dancing in the wok fill the kitchen. Within minutes, you've created a tasty, home-cooked dinner that brings joy to your dinner table.

Or picture a busy midweek evening. You're caught in traffic and by the time you arrive home, you're starving and short on time. Here's where your wok really shines. You can quickly prepare a tasty, colorful dinner that satisfies your appetite without sacrificing flavor or quality with a few simple ingredients and a hot wok.

Then there are days when you're in the mood for adventure and want to try out new flavors and textures. You've purchased a wok and you're curious to see what it can do. With the help of this book, you'll embark on a culinary journey around Asia, discovering fragrant dishes that will take your taste buds to far-off places. Your wok brings up a world of options, from the powerful, spicy notes of Thai cuisine to the subtle, savory tastes of Chinese stir-fries.

With its rich heritage and unmatched adaptability, the wok opens up a world of interesting and approachable culinary opportunities.

What You Can Look Forward To In This Book

In this book, you'll find everything you need to start your journey with wok cooking. From selecting the right wok to mastering essential techniques and creating delicious meals, we've got you covered.

We start with an introduction to the rich history and many advantages of utilizing a wok. You'll discover the benefits of this time-tested cooking technique and how it can elevate your culinary adventures. Selecting the right wok is essential, so we'll walk you through the different types and offer tips on maintenance and seasoning to make sure your wok lasts for many years.

We'll then go over essential wok techniques and ingredients. You'll become an expert in the fundamental techniques such as stir-frying, deep-frying, steaming, and smoking. We'll introduce you to key flavors and staple ingredients that characterize wok dishes, together with providing tips on how to use the best cooking oils and utensils.

If you're pressed for time but still want to enjoy home-cooked meals, our quick and easy weeknight dinners are ideal for you. These recipes can be prepared in 20 minutes or less, making it easy to whip up tasty dinners even on the busiest nights.

Health-conscious readers will like our section on healthy wok cooking. We provide nourishing and delicious recipes that highlight the wok's ability to create light, nutritious meals without sacrificing flavor or texture.

In the versatile wok recipes section, you'll discover a wide variety of meals, including beef, pork, and lamb as well as chicken, duck, seafood, and vegetarian options. We've made sure there's something for everyone by including delicious recipes for noodles, rice, and more.

After building your skills with these varied and delicious meals, we offer some classic recipes for those who want to experiment with great classics from Chinese, Japanese, Thai, and Korean cuisines. These recipes are presented in a beginner-friendly way, providing you with a strong starting point and encouraging you to explore new flavors and techniques

To round out your meals, we've also included delicious salads, essential sauces, quick snacks, and wok-friendly sweet treats. These additions will expand your culinary range and wow your guests.

This book is designed to be your guide as you step into the world of wok cooking. The recipes and culinary tips you'll discover here will help you prepare tasty, delicious meals that you can enjoy preparing for your family, yourself, or your guests. Let's embark on this culinary journey together and experience the joy of wok cooking!

Chapter 1
Getting Started with Wok Cooking

The History of Wok Cooking

Wok cooking has a long and illustrious history that goes back more than 2,000 years to the Chinese Han Dynasty. With its distinctive shape and multipurpose use, the wok (镬, huò) has been an essential part of Asian cooking customs. Woks were first created from cast iron with the purpose of swiftly and effectively cooking meals at high heat. In the past, when food preservation was vital, this practice was very helpful in preserving nutrients and flavours.

The wok traveled with Chinese food throughout Asia and the rest of the world. It still represents quick, wholesome, and delicious cooking today. Cooks who value the wok's versatility and ease of use in the kitchen have made it an indispensable piece of equipment in kitchens around the globe, from street sellers in bustling Asian cities to home kitchens everywhere.

The Benefits of Using a Wok

Why should you consider adding a wok to your kitchen toolkit? Here are a few strong benefits:

1. **Versatility:** A wok is incredibly versatile. You can use it for stir-frying, deep-frying, steaming, smoking, and even braising. This versatility allows you to save time and space in your kitchen by using a single pan for various cooking methods.

2. **Efficiency:** The wok's unique design enables rapid, uniform heating. The food cooks more quickly and evenly because of the sloped sides' effective heat circulation. This is perfect for those busy weeknight dinners when you want to get a meal on the table quickly.

3. **Healthier Cooking**: You may prepare healthier food since woks use less oil when cooking. The nutrients in your meal are also preserved by the high heat and short cooking times.

4. **Flavor Enhancement**: Wok cooking's high heat helps to quickly sear ingredients, locking in flavors and giving meals the distinct smokey flavor known as "wok hei" (镬气, huò qì). This unique flavor, which translates as "breath of the wok," is a defining feature of authentic wok cooking, giving depth and complexity to your meals.

Choosing Your Wok

Selecting the right wok is essential for getting the best cooking experience. Here are some key considerations:

Types of Woks:

Carbon Steel: This is the most widely used material for woks. It is lightweight, heats up evenly, and once seasoned, has a naturally non-stick surface. However, it needs frequent seasoning to maintain its surface.

Cast Iron: Perfect for cooking at high temperatures, these woks hold heat incredibly well. They produce a highly steady cooking temperature, but they are heavier and require longer to heat up. They also require seasoning just like carbon steel.

Non-stick: Non-stick woks are simple to use and maintain, making them perfect for beginners. Although they don't need to be seasoned, their limited heat tolerance makes them less versatile.

Round vs. Flat Bottom: Traditional round-bottom woks function best when used with a wok ring on a gas stove. Flat-bottom woks are a better fit for electric or induction burners because they offer more stability and better contact with the heating element.

How to Season Your Wok

It is very important to season your wok, particularly if it is made of cast iron or carbon steel. This is how you do it:

1. **Clean the Wok**: To get rid of any manufacturing oils, wash your new wok in hot, soapy water. Rinse well and dry thoroughly.
2. **Heat the Wok**: Turn up the heat to high and wait for smoke to appear. This opens the metal's pores.
3. **Put Oil on It**: Drizzle the wok with a small amount of oil, such as vegetable or peanut oil. Spread it evenly across the surface with a paper towel.
4. **Heat Again**: Continue heating the wok until the oil begins to smoke. Once the heat is off, let the wok cool. Repeat this 2-3 more times.
5. **Wipe Clean**: Use a paper towel to wipe the wok, and it's ready for use. The wok will naturally acquire a non-stick surface over time.

Maintenance and Cleaning Tips

Maintaining your wok is easy yet necessary to keep it in good condition:

Everyday Upkeep: Wipe your wok down with a gentle sponge and hot water after each usage. Soap and harsh cleansers should be avoided since they might remove the seasoning.

Deep Cleaning: Use a bamboo brush or non-abrasive scrubber with hot water to clean the wok if food sticks to it or if it takes on a patina. Some salt can be used as a mild abrasive for stubborn residues.

Re-seasoning Tips: Scrub your wok down, give it a thorough washing, and then reseason it if it starts to rust or lose its seasoning.

By being aware of the history, benefits, and maintenance requirements of your wok, you're well on your way to making the most of this useful kitchen tool. Next, we'll get into the key techniques and ingredients that will make wok cooking genuinely remarkable for you.

Chapter 2
Essential Wok Techniques and Ingredients

To master wok cooking, it's essential to get familiar with some key techniques and ingredients that define this style of cooking. Let's explore the fundamental methods you'll use and the flavors that make wok-cooked dishes so distinctive.

Understanding the main techniques and ingredients that characterize wok cooking is crucial to becoming a wok cooking expert. Let's go over the fundamental methods you'll use and the flavors that set wok-cooked food apart.

Essential Wok Techniques

The key to wok cooking is intense heat, quick cooking times, and continuous movement. The following are the four fundamental techniques you should be aware of:

- **Stir-Frying**: Wok cooking is centered around stir-frying. It involves cooking ingredients quickly over high heat while stirring them continually.
- **Preparation**: Make sure all ingredients are cut uniformly for even cooking and dried well to prevent splattering.
- **Heat the Wok**: Preheat your wok until it begins to emit smoke. This avoids sticking and guarantees a nice sear.
- **Oil**: To coat the wok, add a tiny quantity of high smoke point oil, such as canola or peanut, and swirl.
- **Cooking**: Add ingredients gradually according to their cooking times. Put aromatics (such as ginger and garlic) first, followed by proteins, and then veggies. To ensure even cooking, stir continuously.

Deep-Frying: The wok's high edges and even heat distribution make deep-frying in it effective.

- **Oil**: Add enough oil to the wok so that the food is covered, about halfway full.
- **Temperature**:Bring the oil's temperature up to 350–375°F. To keep it stable, use a thermometer.
- **Frying**: To keep the oil at the proper temperature, fry in small batches. Using a spider skimmer, remove the food and drain on paper towels.

Steaming: Steaming in a wok is a healthy method that preserves nutrients.

- **Setup**: Place a steaming rack or bamboo steamer in the wok with water underneath, not touching the food.
- **Heat**: Bring the water to a boil, then lower the heat to a simmer.
- **Steam**: Place food inside the steamer on a heat-resistant platter. Cover and steam until done.

Smoking: Smoking in a wok adds a distinct flavor to dishes.

- **Line the Wok**: Line the bottom with foil to protect the wok.
- **Smoking Materials**: Make use of rice, tea leaves, or wood chips. Place on the foil and heat up until they begin to smoke.
- **Setup**: Arrange the meal on a rack that is placed above the smoking materials. Use extra foil or a lid to cover.
- **Smoke**: Using medium heat, smoke the meal until the desired amount of smokey flavor is absorbed.

Understanding Flavors and Ingredients

Flavor balance is an art form in wok cooking. Here's an overview of the five key flavors and some common ingredients you'll encounter.

Key Flavors:

- **Salty**: Ingredients like soy sauce, fish sauce, and fermented bean paste add depth and enhance other flavors.

- **Sweet**: The subtle sweetness provided by sugar, honey, and hoisin sauce counterbalances the sour and salty flavors.

- **Sour**: Vinegar, tamarind, and citrus juices add a tangy note that enhances foods.

- **Bitter**: Bitter melon and certain greens contribute a nuanced, slightly bitter taste.

- **Umami**: Soy sauce,mushrooms and miso provide a deep, savory flavor that completes a dish.

Common Ingredients:

- **Soy Sauce**: A staple for marinades and sauces, that adds a savory, umami-rich flavor to dishes.

- **Garlic and Ginger**: Essential aromatics that add depth and warmth to a variety of meals.

- **Scallions**: Used as both an ingredient and a garnish, adding a fresh, onion-like taste.

- **Oyster Sauce**: Provides a rich, savory flavor with a hint of sweetness.

- **Rice Wine**: Used in marinades and sauces to add depth and richness.

By learning these techniques and understanding the fundamental flavors and ingredients, you'll be well-equipped to prepare excellent, genuine wok-cooked meals. This chapter establishes a foundation for all of your future work adventures, making the process both pleasant and rewarding.

Essential Tools and Types of Oil

Essential Tools

To get the most out of your wok, you need a few critical items intended to suit its particular shape and cooking style:

- **Wok Spatula**: Designed to suit the curved sides of a wok, this spatula is ideal for swiftly stirring, turning, and tossing ingredients.
- **Ladle**: Perfect for scooping up sauces, soups, and other liquids, as well as for serving.
- **Spider Skimmer**: This gadget is ideal for deep-frying and blanching, as it allows you to securely remove food from hot oil or boiling water.
- **Steaming Rack**: Required for steaming items in your wok, allowing you to benefit from one of the healthiest cooking techniques.

Types of Oil

Because of the high temperatures involved, selecting the appropriate oil is critical for effective wok cooking. Here are some of the top choices:

- **Peanut Oil**: Peanut oil, with its high smoke point and neutral flavor, is an excellent choice for wok cooking. It can withstand the high temperatures used in stir-frying and deep-frying.
- **Canola Oil**: Another great option because of its high smoke point and low cost. It is flexible and abundantly available.
- **Vegetable Oil**: Vegetable oil is a versatile and high-smoke-point oil that is used for a variety of wok cooking techniques.
- **Sesame Oil**: This oil has a lower smoke point and is normally used sparingly due to its strong taste. It is best used at the end of cooking or as a finishing touch on foods.

By stocking your kitchen with these necessary equipment and oils, you'll be fully prepared to tackle any wok recipe with confidence and competence.

Wok Safety Tips and Common Mistakes to Avoid

When cooking with a wok, safety comes first. Here are some essential tips to remember:

First, exercise caution when handling hot oil. Always add ingredients away from you to avoid splatters that can result in burns and messy cleanups. Using long-handled utensils helps keep your hands protected from the intense heat. It's also a good idea to keep a lid nearby in case of a flare-up.

Proper ventilation is essential for a comfortable cooking environment. Make sure your kitchen has adequate ventilation to disperse smoke and steam effectively.

Now, let's look at some common mistakes. Overcrowding the wok is a big one. Adding too many ingredients at once reduces the temperature, causing your food to steam instead of stir-fry. Cook in batches for the perfect sear.

Another mistake is is failing to adequately preheat the wok. A well-preheated wok guarantees that your food sears perfectly and doesn't stick. Before adding the oil, heat the wok until it starts to smoke lightly.

Keep these tips in mind and avoid these common errors, and you'll soon be cooking with confidence. With a little experience, using a wok will feel natural, and you'll be whipping up wonderful dishes without effort.

Chapter 3

Quick and Easy Weeknight Dinners

20-Minute Recipes for Busy Weeknights

We all know the feeling of coming home after a long day, hungry and ready for a delicious meal, but without the energy or time to spend hours in the kitchen. This chapter is dedicated to those busy weeknights when you need something quick, easy, and absolutely tasty. In just 20 minutes, you can whip up a variety of delightful dishes using your trusty wok. These recipes are beginner-friendly and designed to maximize flavor with minimal effort, ensuring you have more time to relax and enjoy your meal.

GARLIC SHRIMP AND VEGETABLE MEDLEY

Servings: 4
Prep Time: 10 minutes
Cook Time: 10 minutes
Total Ingredients: 8

Nutrition Facts (per serving):
Calories: 220 | Fat: 8g | Carbohydrates: 9g | Protein: 28g | Sodium: 540mg | Cholesterol: 170mg

Ingredients:

» 1 lb large shrimp, peeled and deveined
» 2 tablespoons vegetable oil
» 4 cloves garlic, minced
» 1 red bell pepper, thinly sliced
» 1 cup sugar snap peas
» 1 small zucchini, thinly sliced
» 2 tablespoons soy sauce
» 1 tablespoon lemon juice
» Salt and pepper to taste

Preparation:

1. **Prep Ingredients:** Peel and devein the shrimp, mince the garlic, slice the bell pepper and zucchini.

Cooking:

2. **Heat Wok:** Preheat the wok on medium-high until it starts to give off a bit of smoke.
3. **Cook Garlic:** Add the oil and garlic. Stir-fry for 30 seconds until it becomes aromatic.
4. **Add Shrimp:** Stir-fry the shrimp for 2-3 minutes until they turn pink. Take out and place on a dish.
5. **Stir-Fry Veggies:** Add the bell pepper, sugar snap peas, and zucchini to the wok. Stir-fry for 3-4 minutes until tender-crisp.
6. **Combine and Season:** Put the shrimp back into the wok. Add the soy sauce, lemon juice, salt, and pepper. Stir-fry for another minute to combine all the flavors.

Serving:

7. **Serve Hot:** Transfer to a serving dish and enjoy immediately.

TERIYAKI CHICKEN EXPRESS

Servings: 4
Prep Time: 10 minutes
Cook Time: 10 minutes
Total Ingredients: 8

Nutrition Facts (per serving):
Calories: 240 | Fat: 8g | Carbohydrates: 12g | Protein: 30g | Sodium: 600mg | Cholesterol: 90mg

Ingredients:

- » 1 lb chicken breast, thinly sliced
- » 2 tablespoons vegetable oil
- » 3 cloves garlic, minced
- » 1/4 cup teriyaki sauce
- » 1 tablespoon soy sauce
- » 1 tablespoon honey
- » 1 green bell pepper, thinly sliced
- » 1 tablespoon sesame seeds

Preparation:

1. **Prep Ingredients:** Thinly slice the chicken breast and bell pepper, and mince the garlic.

Cooking:

2. **Heat Wok:** Preheat the wok on medium-high until it starts to lightly smoke.
3. **Cook Garlic:** Add the oil and garlic. Stir-fry for 30 seconds until it becomes aromatic.
4. **Add Chicken:** Stir-fry the chicken slices for 3-4 minutes until they are cooked through and no longer pink.
5. **Stir-Fry Veggies:** Add the bell pepper to the wok. Stir-fry for 2-3 minutes until tender-crisp.
6. **Combine and Season:** Add the teriyaki sauce, soy sauce, and honey. Stir-fry for another 1-2 minutes until the chicken and vegetables are well coated and heated through.

Serving:

7. **Garnish and Serve:** Sprinkle with sesame seeds before serving. Enjoy your quick and easy Teriyaki Chicken Express!

SPICY TOFU STIR-FRY

Servings: 4
Prep Time: 10 minutes
Cook Time: 10 minutes
Total Ingredients: 8

Nutrition Facts (per serving):
Calories: 180 | Fat: 10g | Carbohydrates: 10g | Protein: 14g | Sodium: 500mg | Cholesterol: 0mg

Ingredients:

- » 14 oz firm tofu, cubed
- » 2 tablespoons vegetable oil
- » 3 cloves garlic, minced
- » 1 red bell pepper, thinly sliced
- » 2 tablespoons soy sauce
- » 1 tablespoon sriracha sauce
- » 1 tablespoon hoisin sauce
- » 1 tablespoon sesame seeds

Preparation:

1. **Prep Ingredients:** Cube the tofu, mince the garlic, and slice the red bell pepper.

Cooking:

2. **Heat Wok:** Preheat the wok on medium-high until it starts to give off a bit of smoke.
3. **Cook Tofu:** Add the oil and tofu. Stir-fry for 3-4 minutes until golden and slightly crispy.
4. **Add Garlic:** Add the garlic to the wok and stir-fry for 30 seconds until it becomes aromatic.
5. **Stir-Fry Veggies:** Add the red bell pepper. Stir-fry for 2-3 minutes until tender-crisp.
6. **Combine and Season:** Add the soy sauce, sriracha, and hoisin sauce. Stir-fry for 1-2 minutes more until the tofu and vegetables are well coated and heated through.

Serving:

7. **Garnish and Serve:** Sprinkle with sesame seeds before serving. Enjoy your quick and flavorful Spicy Tofu Stir-Fry!

VEGGIE FRIED RICE SPRINT

Servings: 4
Prep Time: 5 minutes
Cook Time: 15 minutes
Total Ingredients: 8

Nutrition Facts (per serving):
Calories: 250 | Fat: 8g | Carbohydrates: 40g | Protein: 5g | Sodium: 500mg | Cholesterol: 0mg

Ingredients:

- » 1 1/2 cups jasmine rice
- » 3 cups water
- » 2 tablespoons vegetable oil
- » 1 small onion, finely chopped
- » 1 cup frozen mixed vegetables ((peas, carrots, green beans)
- » 2 cloves garlic, minced
- » 2 tablespoons soy sauce
- » 1 tablespoon sesame oil
- » 2 green onions, sliced

Preparation:

1. **Cook Rice:** In a medium saucepan, bring 3 cups of water to a boil. Add the jasmine rice, reduce the heat to low, cover, and simmer for 15 minutes or until the rice is tender and all the liquid has been absorbed. Fluff with a fork and set aside.
2. **Prep Ingredients:** While the rice is cooking, chop the onion, mince the garlic, and slice the green onions.

Cooking:

3. **Heat Wok:** Preheat the wok on medium-high until a little smoke starts to appear.
4. **Cook Onion and Veggies:** Add the vegetable oil and chopped onion. Stir-fry for 2-3 minutes until the onion starts to turn clear.
5. **Add Mixed Vegetables:** Toss in the frozen mixed vegetables (peas, carrots, green beans) and minced garlic. Stir-fry for another 2-3 minutes until the vegetables are soft and fragrant.
6. **Add Rice:** Add the cooked rice to the wok. Stir-fry for 3-4 minutes, breaking up any clumps, until the rice is thoroughly cooked and beginning to crisp up.
7. **Season:** Drizzle the soy sauce and sesame oil over the rice. Stir-fry for another minute, ensuring the sauce is distributed evenly over the rice.

Serving:

8. **Garnish and Serve:** Sprinkle with sliced green onions before serving. Enjoy your quick and delicious Veggie Fried Rice Sprint!

BEEF AND SNOW PEA STIR-FRY

Servings: 4
Prep Time: 10 minutes
Cook Time: 10 minutes
Total Ingredients: 8

Nutrition Facts (per serving):
Calories: 280 | Fat: 15g | Carbohydrates: 10g | Protein: 25g | Sodium: 600mg | Cholesterol: 55mg

Ingredients:

- » 1 lb beef sirloin, thinly sliced
- » 2 tablespoons vegetable oil
- » 2 cups snow peas, trimmed
- » 2 cloves garlic, minced
- » 1 tablespoon soy sauce
- » 1 tablespoon oyster sauce
- » 2 tablespoons of water and 1 teaspoon of cornstarch
- » 2 green onions, sliced

Preparation:

1. **Prep Ingredients:** Thinly slice the beef sirloin, trim the snow peas, mince the garlic, and slice the green onions.

Cooking:

2. **Heat Wok:** Preheat the wok on medium-high until it begins to emit a little smoke.
3. **Cook Beef:** Add 1 tablespoon of vegetable oil to the wok. Add the sliced beef and stir-fry for 3-4 minutes until browned and just heated through. Take out the beef from the wok and place it on a plate.
4. **Stir-Fry Vegetables:** Pour the remaining tablespoon of vegetable oil into the wok. Add the snow peas and minced garlic, and stir-fry for 2-3 minutes until the snow peas are tender-crisp.
5. **Combine and Sauce:** Bring the beef back into the wok. Add the soy sauce, oyster sauce, and cornstarch mixture. Stir-fry for 2-3 more minutes until the sauce thickens and everything is well-coated.

Serving:

6. **Garnish and Serve:** Sprinkle with sliced green onions before serving. Enjoy your flavorful Beef and Snow Pea Stir-Fry with steamed rice or noodles.

ZESTY LEMON PEPPER CHICKEN

Servings: 4

Prep Time: 10 minutes

Cook Time: 10 minutes

Total Ingredients: 8

Nutrition Facts (per serving):

Calories: 240 | Fat: 10g | Carbohydrates: 6g | Protein: 30g | Sodium: 450mg | Cholesterol: 75mg

Ingredients:

» 1 lb boneless, skinless chicken breasts, thinly sliced
» 2 tablespoons vegetable oil
» 2 cloves garlic, minced
» 1 bell pepper, thinly sliced
» 1 lemon, zest and juice
» 1 teaspoon black pepper
» 1 tablespoon soy sauce
» 2 green onions, sliced

Preparation:

1. **Prep Ingredients:** Thinly slice the chicken breasts and bell pepper, mince the garlic, zest and juice the lemon, and slice the green onions.

Cooking:

2. **Heat Wok:** Preheat the wok on medium-high until it starts to give off a bit of smoke.
3. **Cook Chicken:** Add 1 tablespoon of vegetable oil to the wok. Add the sliced chicken and stir-fry for 3-4 minutes until cooked through and a little browned. Lift out the chicken from the wok and place on a plate.
4. **Stir-Fry Vegetables:** Pour the remaining tablespoon of vegetable oil into the wok. Add the minced garlic and thinly sliced bell pepper. Stir-fry for 2-3 minutes until the bell pepper is tender-crisp.
5. **Combine and Sauce:** Transfer the chicken back into the wok. Add the lemon zest, lemon juice, black pepper, and soy sauce. Stir-fry for another 2-3 minutes until everything is well cooked and covered.

Serving:

6. **Garnish and Serve:** Sprinkle with sliced green onions before serving. Enjoy your Zesty Lemon Pepper Chicken with steamed rice or a fresh salad.

SWEET CHILI CHICKEN DELIGHT

Servings: 4
Prep Time: 10 minutes
Cook Time: 10 minutes
Total Ingredients: 7

Nutrition Facts (per serving):
Calories: 320 | Fat: 14g | Carbohydrates: 15g | Protein: 30g | Sodium: 600mg | Cholesterol: 70mg

Ingredients:

» 1 lb boneless, skinless chicken breasts, cut into narrow strips
» 2 tablespoons vegetable oil
» 1 yellow bell pepper, thinly sliced
» 1 cup snap peas
» 1/2 cup sweet chili sauce
» 2 tablespoons soy sauce
» 2 green onions, sliced

Preparation:

1. **Prep Ingredients:** Cut the chicken breasts into narrow strips. Slice the yellow bell pepper. Slice the green onions. Prepare the snap peas by trimming the ends.

Cooking:

2. **Heat the Wok:** Put the wok on medium-high and add the vegetable oil. Do not smoke the oil, just make it hot.
3. **Cook Chicken:** Place the chicken strips in the wok and stir-fry them for approximately 5 minutes, or until the chicken is cooked through and the center is no longer pink.
4. **Add Vegetables:** Fill the wok with the snap peas and yellow bell pepper. Stir-fry the veggies for 3 more minutes, or until they become tender-crisp.
5. **Add Sauce:** Pour the sweet chili sauce and soy sauce into the wok. Give the chicken and vegetables a good stir to coat them uniformly. Simmer for a further 2 minutes to give the sauce a slight thickening.

Serving:

6. **Garnish and Serve:** Take it off the heat and add the sliced green onions on top. Serve hot with steamed rice or noodles.

MUSHROOM & BOK CHOY STIR-FRY

Servings: 4
Prep Time: 10 minutes
Cook Time: 10 minutes
Total Ingredients: 7

Nutrition Facts (per serving):
Calories: 120 | Fat: 7g | Carbohydrates: 10g | Protein: 4g | Sodium: 500mg | Cholesterol: 0mg

Ingredients:

» 2 tablespoons vegetable oil
» 1 lb mixed mushrooms (shiitake, button, or cremini), sliced
» 4 cups baby bok choy, halved lengthwise
» 2 cloves garlic, minced
» 2 tablespoons soy sauce
» 1 tablespoon oyster sauce (optional for vegetarians: replace with hoisin sauce)
» 1 teaspoon sesame oil

Preparation:

1. **Prep Ingredients:** Slice the mushrooms and halve the baby bok choy lengthwise. Mince the garlic.

Cooking:

2. **Heat the Wok:** Heat the vegetable oil in a wok over medium-high heat until hot but not smoking.
3. **Cook Mushrooms:** Add the sliced mushrooms to the wok. Stir-fry for 5 minutes, or until they are browned and tender.
4. **Add Garlic and Bok Choy:** Add the minced garlic and baby bok choy to the wok. Stir-fry for 3 more minutes, or until the bok choy is tender but still crisp.
5. **Add Sauces:** Add the soy sauce, oyster sauce, and sesame oil. Give the vegetables a good stir to cover them evenly. Cook for 2 more minutes to combine the flavors.

Serving:

6. **Serve:** Take off the heat and place on a platter. Enjoy your Mushroom & Bok Choy Stir-Fry hot, with steamed rice or as a side to your favorite main dish.

SPEEDY CURRY VEGETABLE MIX

Servings: 4
Prep Time: 10 minutes
Cook Time: 10 minutes
Total Ingredients: 8

Nutrition Facts (per serving):
Calories: 150 | Fat: 9g | Carbohydrates: 15g | Protein: 3g | Sodium: 550mg | Cholesterol: 0mg

Ingredients:

»   2 tablespoons vegetable oil
»   1 yellow bell pepper, thinly sliced
»   1 zucchini, thinly sliced
»   1 carrot, julienned
»   2 cloves garlic, minced
»   1 tablespoon curry powder
»   2 tablespoons soy sauce
»   1/2 cup coconut milk

Preparation:

1. **Prep Ingredients:** Thinly slice the bell pepper and zucchini. Julienne the carrot and mince the garlic.

Cooking:

2. **Heat the Wok:** Over medium-high heat, heat the vegetable oil in a wok until it's hot but not smoking.
3. **Cook Vegetables:** Add the bell pepper, zucchini, and carrot to the wok. Stir-fry for 5 minutes, or until the vegetables are tender-crisp.
4. **Add Garlic and Curry Powder:** Add the minced garlic and curry powder to the wok. Stir well to coat the vegetables and cook for 1-2 more minutes until the aroma is released.
5. **Add Sauces:** Add the soy sauce and coconut milk. Stir well to combine, and cook for another 2 minutes until the sauce is hot and slightly thickened.

Serving:

6. **Serve:** Take off the heat and transfer to a platter. Enjoy your Speedy Curry Vegetable Mix hot, with noodles or steamed rice.

HONEY SOY GLAZED SALMON

Servings: 4
Prep Time: 10 minutes
Cook Time: 10 minutes
Total Ingredients: 7

Nutrition Facts (per serving):
Calories: 320 | Fat: 14g | Carbohydrates: 12g | Protein: 34g | Sodium: 540mg | Cholesterol: 70mg

Ingredients:

» 4 salmon fillets (about 1 lb total)
» 2 tablespoons soy sauce
» 2 tablespoons honey
» 2 cloves garlic
» 1 tablespoon vegetable oil
» 1 teaspoon fresh ginger
» 2 green onions, sliced (for garnish)

Preparation:

1. **Prep Ingredients:** Mince the garlic and grate the fresh ginger.
2. **Prepare the Marinade:** In a small bowl, combine soy sauce, honey, minced garlic, and grated fresh ginger until well combined.

Cooking:

3. **Heat the Wok:** Preheat the wok on medium-high until it begins to emit a little smoke.
4. **Cook the Salmon:** Add vegetable oil to the wok. Put the salmon fillets in the wok, skin side down if applicable. Cook for 3-4 minutes, then flip and cook for another 3-4 minutes, or until the salmon is well cooked and readily flaked with a fork.
5. **Add the Glaze:** Pour the honey-soy mixture over the salmon fillets in the last 2 minutes of cooking. Spoon the glaze over the fillets to coat them well, allowing it to thicken slightly.

Serving:

6. **Garnish and Serve:** Remove the salmon from the wok and place it on a dish for serving. Garnish with sliced green onions and serve immediately. Enjoy your Honey Soy Glazed Salmon with steamed rice or a side of sautéed vegetables.

SESAME CHICKEN AND ASPARAGUS STIR-FRY

Servings: 4
Prep Time: 10 minutes
Cook Time: 10 minutes
Total Ingredients: 8

Nutrition Facts (per serving):
Calories: 290 | Fat: 12g | Carbohydrates: 10g | Protein: 32g | Sodium: 620mg | Cholesterol: 85mg

Ingredients:

» 1 lb boneless, skinless chicken breasts
» 1 bunch asparagus, trimmed and cut into 2-inch pieces
» 2 tablespoons soy sauce
» 1 tablespoon sesame oil
» 1 tablespoon vegetable oil
» 1 tablespoon honey
» 2 cloves garlic, minced
» 1 tablespoon sesame seeds (for garnish)

Preparation:

1. **Prep Ingredients:** Thinly slice the chicken breasts. Trim and cut the asparagus into 2-inch pieces. Mince the garlic.
2. **Prepare the Sauce:** In a small bowl, mix together sesame oil, honey, soy sauce and minced garlic until well combined.

Cooking:

3. **Heat the Wok:** Preheat the wok on medium-high until it begins to emit a little smoke.
4. **Cook the Chicken:** Add vegetable oil to the wok. Add the sliced chicken and stir-fry for 4-5 minutes, or until the chicken is well cooked and lightly browned.
5. **Add Asparagus:** Add the asparagus to the wok and stir-fry for 3-4 minutes, until tender-crisp.
6. **Add the Sauce:** Pour the sesame sauce over the chicken and asparagus. Stir-fry for another 1-2 minutes, making sure the sauce coats everything well.

Serving:

7. **Garnish and Serve:** Take off the heat and place on a platter. Serve right away after adding sesame seeds as a garnish. Enjoy your Sesame Chicken and Asparagus Stir-Fry with steamed rice or noodles.

QUICK CASHEW CHICKEN FUSION

Servings: 4
Prep Time: 10 minutes
Cook Time: 10 minutes
Total Ingredients: 8

Nutrition Facts (per serving):
Calories: 350 | Fat: 18g | Carbohydrates: 12g | Protein: 30g | Sodium: 620mg | Cholesterol: 60mg

Ingredients:

» 1 lb boneless, skinless chicken breasts
» 1 cup unsalted cashews
» 2 tablespoons vegetable oil
» 1 red bell pepper
» 1 green bell pepper
» 3 tablespoons soy sauce
» 2 tablespoons hoisin sauce
» 2 green onions

Preparation:

1. **Prep Ingredients:** Dice the chicken breasts, thinly slice the red and green bell peppers, and slice the green onions.

Cooking:

2. **Heat the Wok:** Preheat the wok on medium-high until it starts to give off a bit of smoke.
3. **Cook the Chicken:** Add 1 tablespoon of vegetable oil to the wok. Add the diced chicken and stir-fry for 4-5 minutes until the chicken is cooked through and slightly browned. Lift the chicken out of the wok and place it on a plate.
4. **Stir-Fry Vegetables and Cashews:** Add the last tablespoon of vegetable oil to the wok. Stir in the thinly sliced bell peppers and cashews. Stir-fry for 2-3 minutes until the bell peppers are tender-crisp.
5. **Combine and Sauce:** Place the chicken back in the wok. Add the soy sauce and hoisin sauce. Stir-fry for another 1-2 minutes until everything is well cooked and covered.

Serving:

6. **Garnish and Serve:** Sprinkle with sliced green onions before serving. Enjoy your Quick Cashew Chicken Stir-Fry with steamed rice or noodles.

Chapter 4
Healthy Wok Cooking

Light and Nutritious Wok Recipes

Welcome to the world of healthy wok cooking, where creating light, nutritious, and delicious meals is both easy and enjoyable. In this chapter, we've chosen recipes that prioritize health using fresh ingredients, lean proteins, and heart-healthy fats. Our goal is to help you enjoy all the benefits of wok cooking while sticking to a healthy diet.

Tips for Healthier Wok Dishes:

1. **Choose Lean Proteins:** Opt for lean cuts of meat like chicken breast, turkey, or fish. Plant-based proteins like tofu, tempeh, and legumes are also excellent choices.
2. **Increase Vegetable Intake:** Load up on a variety of colorful vegetables to add fiber, vitamins, and minerals while keeping calories low.
3. **Use Healthy Oils:** Select oils with high smoke points and health benefits, such as olive oil, avocado oil, or sesame oil, and use them sparingly.
4. **Control Portion Sizes:** Be mindful of portion sizes to avoid overeating. Balanced meals with appropriate portions of protein, vegetables, and whole grains are key.
5. **Reduce Sodium:** Use low-sodium soy sauce and broths. Enhance flavor with herbs, spices, and citrus instead of relying heavily on salt.
6. **Add Whole Grains:** Serve your stir-fries with whole grains like brown rice, quinoa, or whole grain noodles for added fiber and nutrients.
7. **Limit Added Sugars:** Be cautious with sauces that contain added sugars. Opt for natural sweeteners like honey or use fruits to add sweetness.
8. **Mind the Cooking Time:** Overcooking vegetables can lead to nutrient loss. Stir-fry vegetables until just tender-crisp to retain their nutritional value and vibrant color.

By following these tips, you can enjoy all the benefits of wok cooking while maintaining a healthy and balanced diet. We have followed this approach while selecting these recipes for you. Now, let's get started with some delicious recipes that are as good for your health as they are for your palate.

LEMON HERB CHICKEN AND GREEN BEANS STIR-FRY

Servings: 4

Prep Time: 15 minutes (including marinating time)

Cook Time: 10 minutes

Total Ingredients: 8

Nutrition Facts (per serving):

Calories: 250 | Fat: 10g | Carbohydrates: 8g | Protein: 28g | Sodium: 450mg | Cholesterol: 75mg

Ingredients:

» 1 lb boneless, skinless chicken breasts, thinly sliced
» 2 tablespoons vegetable oil
» 3 cloves garlic, minced
» 1 lemon, zest and juice
» 1 teaspoon dried oregano
» 1 teaspoon dried thyme
» 2 cups green beans, trimmed
» Salt and pepper to taste

Preparation:

1. **Marinate the Chicken:** In a mixing bowl, combine the sliced chicken with lemon zest, lemon juice, dried oregano, dried thyme, salt, and pepper. Mix well and let it marinate for 5-10 minutes.

Cooking:

2. **Heat the Wok:** Preheat the wok over medium-high heat until it is hot and just begins to smoke.
3. **Cook Chicken:** Add 1 tablespoon of vegetable oil to the wok. Add the marinated chicken and stir-fry for 4-5 minutes until it is cooked through and slightly browned. Lift the chicken from the wok and place on a dish.
4. **Stir-Fry Vegetables:** Add the remaining tablespoon of vegetable oil to the wok. Add the minced garlic and stir-fry for 30 seconds until aromatic.
5. **Add Green Beans:** Add the trimmed green beans and stir-fry for 3-4 minutes until tender-crisp.
6. **Combine and Finish the Dish:** Place the chicken back in the wok. Stir-fry for 2 more minutes to blend the flavors and ensure everything is well cooked.

Serving:

7. **Serve:** Transfer the Lemon Herb Chicken and Green Beans Stir-Fry to a serving dish. Serve immediately with steamed rice or quinoa for a complete meal. Enjoy your healthy and flavorful creation!

TOFU AND ZUCCHINI STIR-FRY

Servings: 4
Prep Time: 5 minutes
Cook Time: 10 minutes
Total Ingredients: 8

Nutrition Facts (per serving):
Calories: 180 | Fat: 9g | Carbohydrates: 12g | Protein: 14g | Sodium: 500mg | Cholesterol: 0mg

Ingredients:

» 1 block (14 oz) firm tofu, drained and cubed
» 2 zucchinis, sliced
» 1 cup baby corn
» 2 tablespoons vegetable oil
» 3 cloves garlic, minced
» 1 tablespoon soy sauce
» 1 tablespoon sriracha sauce
» 1 teaspoon sesame oil
» 2 green onions, sliced

Preparation:

1. **Prep Ingredients:** Drain and cube the tofu. Slice the zucchinis and baby corn. Mince the garlic. Slice the green onions.

Cooking:

2. **Heat the Wok:** Preheat the wok on medium-high until it begins to produce a little smoke.
3. **Cook Tofu:** Add 1 tablespoon of vegetable oil to the wok. Add the cubed tofu and stir-fry for 4-5 minutes until golden brown and crispy on all sides. Take the tofu out of the wok and place it on a dish.
4. **Stir-Fry Vegetables:** Pour the remaining tablespoon of vegetable oil to the wok. Add the minced garlic, sliced zucchinis, and baby corn. Stir-fry for 3-4 minutes until the vegetables are tender-crisp.
5. **Combine and Sauce:** Bring the tofu back to the wok. Add the soy sauce, sriracha sauce, and sesame oil. Stir-fry for 2-3 more minutes until all ingredients are well cooked and covered.

Serving:

6. **Garnish and Serve:** Sprinkle with sliced green onions before serving. Enjoy your Tofu and Zucchini Stir-Fry with a side of steamed rice or quinoa for a complete meal.

GINGER SHRIMP AND BROCCOLI STIR-FRY

Servings: 4
Prep Time: 5 minutes
Cook Time: 10 minutes
Total Ingredients: 8

Nutrition Facts (per serving):
Calories: 220 | Fat: 10g | Carbohydrates: 9g | Protein: 23g | Sodium: 600mg | Cholesterol: 140mg

Ingredients:

» 1 lb large shrimp, peeled and deveined
» 2 cups broccoli florets
» 2 tablespoons vegetable oil
» 3 cloves garlic, minced
» 1 tablespoon fresh ginger, minced
» 2 tablespoons soy sauce
» 1 tablespoon oyster sauce
» 1 teaspoon sesame oil

Preparation:

1. **Prep Ingredients:** Peel and devein the shrimp. Cut the broccoli into florets. Mince the garlic and fresh ginger.

Cooking:

2. **Heat the Wok:** Preheat the wok on medium-high until it starts to produce a bit of smoke.
3. **Cook Shrimp:** Add 1 tablespoon of vegetable oil to the wok. Add the shrimp and stir-fry for 2-3 minutes until they turn pink and are just cooked through. Remove the shrimp from the wok and set aside.
4. **Stir-Fry Vegetables:** Pour the remaining tablespoon of vegetable oil to the wok. Add the minced garlic and ginger, stir-fry for 1 minute until aromatic. Add the broccoli florets and stir-fry for 3-4 minutes until they are tender-crisp.
5. **Combine and Sauce:** Bring the shrimp back into the wok. Add the soy sauce, oyster sauce, and sesame oil. Stir-fry for another 2-3 minutes until everything is heated through and well covered.

Serving:

6. **Garnish and Serve:** Serve your Ginger Shrimp and Broccoli Stir-Fry hot, over a bed of steamed rice or quinoa. Enjoy the vibrant flavors and healthy goodness of this easy weeknight meal.

MISO-GLAZED VEGETABLE MEDLEY

Servings: 4

Prep Time: 5 minutes

Cook Time: 10 minutes

Total Ingredients: 8

Nutrition Facts (per serving):

Calories: 180 | Fat: 7g | Carbohydrates: 23g | Protein: 4g | Sodium: 600mg | Cholesterol: 0mg

Ingredients:

- » 2 cups broccoli florets
- » 1 red bell pepper, sliced
- » 1 yellow bell pepper, sliced
- » 1 zucchini, sliced
- » 2 tablespoons vegetable oil
- » 2 tablespoons miso paste
- » 2 tablespoons mirin
- » 1 tablespoon soy sauce

Preparation:

1. **Prep Vegetables:** Cut the broccoli into florets. Slice the red and yellow bell peppers. Slice the zucchini.

Cooking:

2. **Heat the Wok:** Preheat the wok on medium-high until it starts to produce a bit of smoke.
3. **Stir-Fry Vegetables:** Add the vegetable oil to the wok. Add the broccoli florets, bell peppers, and zucchini. Stir-fry for 5-6 minutes until the vegetables are tender-crisp.
4. **Prepare Miso Glaze:** In a small bowl, combine the mirin, miso paste and soy sauce until well blended.
5. **Combine and Glaze:** Pour the miso glaze over the vegetables in the wok. Stir-fry for another 2-3 minutes until the vegetables are evenly coated and the glaze is heated through.

Serving:

6. **Serve:** Serve your Miso-Glazed Vegetable Medley hot, as a main dish or a side dish. Enjoy the rich umami flavors and the fresh, vibrant vegetables.

QUINOA AND EDAMAME STIR-FRY WITH SESAME SAUCE

Servings: 4
Prep Time: 10 minutes
Cook Time: 15 minutes
Total Ingredients: 8

Nutrition Facts (per serving):
Calories: 250 | Fat: 9g | Carbohydrates: 30g | Protein: 10g | Sodium: 550mg | Cholesterol: 0mg

Ingredients:

» 1 cup quinoa, cooked
» 1 cup shelled edamame
» 1 red bell pepper, sliced
» 1 carrot, julienned
» 2 tablespoons vegetable oil
» 2 tablespoons soy sauce
» 1 tablespoon sesame oil
» 1 tablespoon sesame seeds

Preparation:

1. **Prep Ingredients:** Cook the quinoa according to package instructions. Slice the red bell pepper and julienne the carrot.

Cooking:

2. **Heat the Wok:** Preheat the wok on medium-high until it starts to give off a bit of smoke.
3. **Stir-Fry Vegetables:** Add the vegetable oil to the wok. Add the bell pepper, carrot, and edamame. Stir-fry for 5-6 minutes until the vegetables are tender-crisp.
4. **Combine Quinoa and Vegetables:** Add the cooked quinoa to the wok. Stir to combine with the vegetables.
5. **Prepare Sesame Sauce:** In a small bowl, blend the soy sauce and sesame oil until well combined.
6. **Sauce and Stir:** Pour the sesame sauce over the quinoa and vegetables in the wok. Stir-fry for another 2-3 minutes until everything is well covered and heated through.

Serving:

7. **Serve:** Sprinkle with sesame seeds before serving. Enjoy your Quinoa and Edamame Stir-Fry with Sesame Sauce as a nutritious main dish or a hearty side.

LIGHT AND SPICY BEEF LETTUCE WRAPS

Servings: 4
Prep Time: 10 minutes
Cook Time: 10 minutes
Total Ingredients: 8

Nutrition Facts (per serving):
Calories: 280 | Fat: 14g | Carbohydrates: 12g | Protein: 25g | Sodium: 600mg | Cholesterol: 70mg

Ingredients:

» 1 lb lean ground beef
» 2 tablespoons vegetable oil
» 1 red bell pepper, diced
» 2 cloves garlic, minced
» 2 tablespoons soy sauce
» 1 tablespoon sriracha or hot sauce
» 1 tablespoon rice vinegar
» 1 head butter lettuce, leaves separated

Preparation:

1. **Prep Ingredients:** Dice the red bell pepper and mince the garlic. Separate and wash the lettuce leaves.

Cooking:

2. **Heat the Wok:** Preheat the wok on medium-high until it starts to give off a bit of smoke.
3. **Cook Beef:** Pour the vegetable oil into the heated wok. Add the ground beef and cook, using a spatula to break it apart, until it is fully browned and cooked through, approximately 5-7 minutes.
4. **Add Vegetables:** Add the minced garlic and diced red bell pepper to the wok. Stir-fry for another 2-3 minutes until the vegetables are soft.
5. **Season:** Add the soy sauce, sriracha, and rice vinegar to the wok. Stir to combine and cook for another 1-2 minutes until the beef mixture is well-coated and heated through.

Serving:

6. **Assemble Wraps:** Spoon the beef mixture into the center of each lettuce leaf.
7. **Serve:** Serve the lettuce wraps immediately, letting everyone assemble their own. Enjoy your Light and Spicy Beef Lettuce Wraps as a refreshing and healthy meal.

GARLIC MUSHROOM AND KALE STIR-FRY

Servings: 4
Prep Time: 5 minutes
Cook Time: 10 minutes
Total Ingredients: 8

Nutrition Facts (per serving):
Calories: 150 | Fat: 10g | Carbohydrates: 10g | Protein: 5g | Sodium: 350mg | Cholesterol: 0mg

Ingredients:

- » 1 tablespoon vegetable oil
- » 2 cloves garlic, minced
- » 1 lb mushrooms, sliced
- » 1 bunch kale, stems removed and leaves chopped
- » 2 tablespoons soy sauce
- » 1 tablespoon rice vinegar
- » 1 teaspoon sesame oil
- » 1/2 teaspoon red pepper flakes (optional)

Preparation:

1. **Prep Ingredients:** Mince the garlic, slice the mushrooms, and chop the kale leaves after removing the stems.

Cooking:

2. **Heat the Wok:** Preheat the wok on medium-high until it starts to give off a bit of smoke.
3. **Cook Garlic:** Add the vegetable oil to the wok. Add the minced garlic and stir-fry for 30 seconds until aromatic.
4. **Add Mushrooms:** Add the sliced mushrooms to the wok. Stir-fry for 3-4 minutes until they begin to release their juices and soften.
5. **Add Kale:** Add the chopped kale to the wok. Stir-fry for 2-3 minutes until the kale wilts and reaches desired tenderness.
6. **Season:** Add the soy sauce, rice vinegar, sesame oil, and red pepper flakes (if using) to the wok. Stir to combine and cook for another 1-2 minutes until everything is well cooked and coated.

Serving:

7. **Serve:** Place the stir-fry onto a platter and enjoy your Garlic Mushroom and Kale Stir-Fry as a nutritious side or a light main dish.

SWEET AND SPICY CARROT AND SNOW PEA QUINOA STIR-FRY

Servings: 4
Prep Time: 10 minutes
Cook Time: 15 minutes
Total Ingredients: 8

Nutrition Facts (per serving):
Calories: 240 | Fat: 8g | Carbohydrates: 32g | Protein: 6g | Sodium: 450mg | Cholesterol: 0mg

Ingredients:

- » 1 tablespoon vegetable oil
- » 2 large carrots, julienned
- » 1 cup snow peas, trimmed
- » 1/4 cup sweet chili sauce
- » 1 tablespoon soy sauce
- » 2 cloves garlic, minced
- » 1 teaspoon grated ginger
- » 1 cup cooked quinoa

Preparation:

1. **Prep Ingredients:** Julienne the carrots, trim the snow peas, mince the garlic, and cook the quinoa following the package instructions.

Cooking:

2. **Heat the Wok:** Preheat the wok on medium-high until it begins to give off a bit of smoke.
3. **Stir-Fry Vegetables:** Add the vegetable oil to the wok. Add the julienned carrots, snow peas, minced garlic, and grated ginger. Stir-fry for 3-4 minutes until the vegetables are tender-crisp.
4. **Combine and Sauce:** Add the sweet chili sauce and soy sauce to the wok. Stir-fry for another 2-3 minutes until everything is well cooked and covered.
5. **Add Quinoa:** Add the cooked quinoa to the wok and toss to combine, heating it through for another 1-2 minutes.

Serving:

6. **Serve:** Enjoy your Sweet and Spicy Carrot and Snow Pea Quinoa Stir-Fry for a flavorful and balanced meal.

THAI-INSPIRED COCONUT LIME CHICKEN STIR-FRY

Servings: 4
Prep Time: 5 minutes
Cook Time: 10 minutes
Total Ingredients: 8

Nutrition Facts (per serving):
Calories: 250 | Fat: 12g | Carbohydrates: 10g | Protein: 25g | Sodium: 400mg | Cholesterol: 70mg

Ingredients:

» 1 tablespoon coconut oil
» 1 lb boneless, skinless chicken breasts, thinly sliced
» 1 red bell pepper, thinly sliced
» 1 cup coconut milk
» 2 tablespoons lime juice
» 2 tablespoons soy sauce
» 1 tablespoon fish sauce
» 1/4 cup fresh cilantro, chopped

Preparation:

1. **Prep Ingredients:** Thinly slice the chicken breasts and red bell pepper. Chop the fresh cilantro.

Cooking:

2. **Heat the Wok:** Preheat the wok on medium-high until it begins to give off a bit of smoke.
3. **Cook Chicken:** Add the coconut oil to the wok. Add the sliced chicken and stir-fry for 3-4 minutes until cooked through and slightly browned. Lift the chicken from the wok and place it on a dish.
4. **Stir-Fry Vegetables:** Put the thinly sliced red bell pepper into the wok. Stir-fry for 2-3 minutes until tender-crisp.
5. **Combine and Sauce:** Place the chicken back into the wok. Add the coconut milk, lime juice, soy sauce, and fish sauce. Stir-fry for another 2-3 minutes until all ingredients are cooked through.

Serving:

6. **Garnish and Serve:** Sprinkle with fresh cilantro before serving. Enjoy your Thai-Inspired Coconut Lime Chicken Stir-Fry with steamed rice or rice noodles.

TERIYAKI CHICKEN AND CAULIFLOWER RICE STIR-FRY

Servings: 4
Prep Time: 5 minutes
Cook Time: 10 minutes
Total Ingredients: 9

Nutrition Facts (per serving):
Calories: 300 | Fat: 10g | Carbohydrates: 15g | Protein: 28g | Sodium: 450mg | Cholesterol: 75mg

Ingredients:

- » 1 tablespoon vegetable oil
- » 1 lb boneless, skinless chicken breasts, diced
- » 1 head of cauliflower, grated into rice-sized pieces
- » 1 red bell pepper, thinly sliced
- » 1 cup snap peas, trimmed
- » 1/4 cup low-sodium teriyaki sauce
- » 2 green onions, sliced
- » 1 tablespoon sesame seeds (optional)
- » 1 teaspoon grated ginger

Preparation:

1. **Prep Ingredients:** Dice the chicken breasts, grate the cauliflower, thinly slice the green onions and red bell pepper and trim the snap peas.

Cooking:

2. **Heat the Wok:** Preheat the wok on medium-high until it starts to give off a bit of smoke.
3. **Cook Chicken:** Add the vegetable oil to the wok. Add the diced chicken and stir-fry for 4-5 minutes until cooked through and slightly browned. Take the chicken from the wok and place on a separate plate.
4. **Stir-Fry Vegetables:** Add the grated cauliflower, red bell pepper, snap peas, and grated ginger to the wok. Stir-fry for 3-4 minutes until the vegetables are tender-crisp.
5. **Combine and Sauce:** Bring the chicken back into the wok. Add the teriyaki sauce and stir-fry for another 2-3 minutes until all parts are cooked and well-coated.

Serving:

6. **Garnish and Serve:** Sprinkle with sliced green onions and sesame seeds (if using) before serving. Enjoy your Teriyaki Chicken and Cauliflower Rice Stir-Fry for a healthy and delicious meal.

SZECHUAN GREEN BEAN AND TOFU STIR-FRY

Servings: 4
Prep Time: 5 minutes
Cook Time: 10 minutes
Total Ingredients: 8

Nutrition Facts (per serving):
Calories: 210 | Fat: 12g | Carbohydrates: 14g | Protein: 12g | Sodium: 540mg | Cholesterol: 0mg

Ingredients:

- » 1 lb green beans, trimmed
- » 1 block (14 oz) firm tofu, cubed
- » 2 tablespoons vegetable oil
- » 2 cloves garlic, minced
- » 1 tablespoon Szechuan peppercorns, crushed
- » 3 tablespoons soy sauce
- » 1 tablespoon rice vinegar
- » 1 tablespoon hoisin sauce

Preparation:

1. **Prep Ingredients:** Trim the green beans, cube the tofu, and mince the garlic.

Cooking:

2. **Heat the Wok:** Preheat the wok on medium-high until it starts to give off a bit of smoke.
3. **Cook the Tofu:** Add 1 tablespoon of vegetable oil to the wok. Add the cubed tofu and stir-fry for 4-5 minutes until golden brown. Lift the tofu from the wok and place it on a dish.
4. **Stir-Fry Green Beans:** Add the remaining tablespoon of vegetable oil to the wok. Add the minced garlic and crushed Szechuan peppercorns. Stir-fry for 1 minute until aromatic.
5. **Combine and Sauce:** Add the green beans to the wok and stir-fry for 2-3 minutes until tender-crisp. Bring the tofu back into the wok. Add the soy sauce, rice vinegar, and hoisin sauce. Stir-fry for 1-2 additional minutes.

Serving:

6. **Serve:** Place on a serving platter and enjoy your Szechuan Green Bean and Tofu Stir-Fry with a side of brown rice or quinoa for a healthy, balanced meal.

LEMON-GARLIC SHRIMP AND ZUCCHINI STIR-FRY

Servings: 4
Prep Time: 5 minutes
Cook Time: 10 minutes
Total Ingredients: 8

Nutrition Facts (per serving):
Calories: 220 | Fat: 10g | Carbohydrates: 8g | Protein: 22g | Sodium: 560mg | Cholesterol: 170mg

Ingredients:

- » 1 lb large shrimp, peeled and deveined
- » 2 medium zucchinis, sliced
- » 2 tablespoons olive oil
- » 3 cloves garlic, minced
- » 1 lemon, zest and juice
- » 1 tablespoon soy sauce
- » 1 teaspoon red pepper flakes
- » 2 green onions, sliced (for garnish)

Preparation:

1. **Prep Ingredients:** Peel and devein the shrimp, slice the zucchinis, mince the garlic, zest and juice the lemon, and slice the green onions.

Cooking:

2. **Heat the Wok:** Preheat the wok on medium-high until it starts to produce a bit of smoke.
3. **Cook the Shrimp:** Add 1 tablespoon of olive oil to the wok. Add the shrimp and stir-fry for 2-3 minutes until pink and opaque. Lift the shrimp from the wok and place them on a dish.
4. **Stir-Fry Zucchini:** Add the remaining tablespoon of olive oil to the wok. Add the minced garlic and stir-fry for 1 minute until fragrant.
5. **Combine and Sauce:** Add the sliced zucchinis to the wok and stir-fry for 2-3 minutes until tender-crisp. Bring the shrimp back into the wok. Add the lemon zest, lemon juice, soy sauce, and red pepper flakes. Stir-fry for 1-2 more minutes.

Serving:

6. **Garnish and Serve:** Sprinkle with sliced green onions before serving. Enjoy your Lemon-Garlic Shrimp and Zucchini Stir-Fry with a side of steamed brown rice or a fresh green salad for a healthy, flavorful meal.

Chapter 5
Versatile Wok Recipes

Welcome to Chapter 5: Versatile Wok Recipes, where we explore a diverse array of dishes that showcase the incredible flexibility of wok cooking. This chapter is designed to inspire you to experiment with various ingredients and techniques, proving that the wok is not just for stir-fries but is a versatile tool for all kinds of culinary adventures.

From hearty beef, pork, and lamb dishes to flavorful chicken and duck recipes, we cover a wide range of proteins to suit any palate. You'll also find an exciting selection of rice and noodle recipes that highlight the comforting and satisfying nature of Asian cuisine. Vegetables, tofu, and egg rolls are not forgotten, offering delicious and nutritious options for those looking to incorporate more plant-based meals into their diet. Finally, our fish and seafood section brings the fresh, vibrant flavors of the ocean to your table.

Whether you're cooking a quick weeknight dinner or preparing an elaborate feast, these recipes will help you make the most of your wok. Each section is packed with dishes that are easy to prepare and full of flavor, ensuring that you'll find something to suit any occasion or craving. So, heat up your wok and get ready to create some unforgettable meals!

SIZZLING MONGOLIAN BEEF STIR-FRY

Servings: 4

Prep Time: 20 minutes (including marinating time of 10 minutes)

Cook Time: 15 minutes

Total Ingredients: 9

Nutrition Facts (per serving):

Calories: 320 | Fat: 15g | Carbohydrates: 20g | Protein: 25g | Sodium: 600mg | Cholesterol: 65mg

Ingredients:

» 1 lb flank steak, thinly sliced
» 2 tablespoons soy sauce
» 1 tablespoon cornstarch
» 3 tablespoons vegetable oil, divided
» 1/2 cup low-sodium soy sauce
» 1/4 cup brown sugar
» 3 cloves garlic, minced
» 1 tablespoon fresh ginger, minced
» 2 green onions, sliced

Preparation:

1. **Marinate the Beef:** In a bowl, toss the thinly sliced flank steak with soy sauce and cornstarch. Let it marinate for 10 minutes.

Cooking:

2. **Prepare the Sauce:** In a small bowl, blend the low-sodium soy sauce and brown sugar until the sugar dissolves.
3. **Stir-Fry the Beef:** Heat 2 tablespoons of vegetable oil in the wok over high heat. Once the oil is hot, add the marinated beef. Stir-fry until the beef is browned and cooked through, approximately 5-6 minutes. Transfer the beef to a plate and set aside.
4. **Cook the Aromatics:** Pour the remaining tablespoon of vegetable oil into the wok. Add the minced garlic and ginger, stir-frying for 30 seconds until aromatic.
5. **Combine Ingredients:** Bring the beef back into the wok, pour in the mixture of soy sauce, and stir well to coat the beef. Cook for another 2-3 minutes until the consistency of the sauce starts to thicken a bit.
6. **6. Finish with Green Onions:** Add the sliced green onions and stir for an additional minute.

Serving:

7. **Serve Immediately:** Transfer the Mongolian beef to a serving dish. Serve hot over noodles or steamed rice, and enjoy your Sizzling Mongolian Beef Stir-Fry!

GINGER PORK STIR-FRY

Servings: 4

Prep Time: 20 minutes (including marinating time of 10 minutes)

Cook Time: 15 minutes

Total Ingredients: 8

Nutrition Facts (per serving):
Calories: 290 | Fat: 12g | Carbohydrates: 15g | Protein: 26g | Sodium: 550mg | Cholesterol: 60mg

Ingredients:

» 1 lb pork tenderloin, thinly sliced
» 2 tablespoons soy sauce
» 1 tablespoon cornstarch
» 3 tablespoons vegetable oil, divided
» 1 red bell pepper, thinly sliced
» 3 cloves garlic, minced
» 2 tablespoons fresh ginger, minced
» 2 green onions, sliced

Preparation:

1. **Marinate the Pork:** In a bowl, toss the thinly sliced pork tenderloin with soy sauce and cornstarch. Let it marinate for 10 minutes.

Cooking:

2. **Stir-Fry the Pork:** Heat 2 tablespoons of vegetable oil in the wok over high heat. Add the marinated pork and cook, stirring frequently, until it is browned and just cooked through, about 5-6 minutes. Lift the pork out of the wok and place it on a dish.

3. **Cook the Vegetables:** Add the last tablespoon of vegetable oil to the wok. Add the chopped garlic and ginger, stir-frying for 30 seconds until fragrant. Fry the red bell pepper slices for 2-3 minutes until they are soft but still crisp.

4. **Combine Ingredients:** Place the pork back into the wok and mix well. Cook for 2-3 more minutes until everything is cooked and well mixed.

Serving:

5. **Serve Immediately:** Transfer the ginger pork stir-fry to a platter. Garnish with sliced green onions and serve hot over steamed rice or noodles. Enjoy your Ginger Pork Stir-Fry!

HONEY GARLIC PORK RIBS

Servings: 4

Prep Time: 1 hour 10 minutes (including marinating time of 1 hour)

Cook Time: 1 hour 30 minutes

Total Ingredients: 9

Nutrition Facts (per serving):
Calories: 450 | Fat: 25g | Carbohydrates: 20g | Protein: 35g | Sodium: 700mg | Cholesterol: 90mg

Ingredients:

» 2 lbs pork ribs, cut into individual ribs
» 1/4 cup soy sauce
» 1/4 cup honey
» 4 cloves garlic, minced
» 1 tablespoon rice vinegar
» 2 tablespoons hoisin sauce
» 1 tablespoon vegetable oil
» 1 teaspoon sesame seeds (for garnish)
» 2 green onions, sliced (for garnish)

Preparation:

1. **Prepare the Marinade:** In a bowl, mix together soy sauce, honey, minced garlic, rice vinegar, and hoisin sauce until well combined.
2. **Marinate the Ribs:** Put the pork ribs in a large zip lock bag or in a shallow container. Drizzle the marinade over the ribs, making sure they are well covered. Seal the bag or cover the container and refrigerate for at least 1 hour, ideally for the entire night to enhance the flavor.

Cooking:

3. **Preheat the Wok:** Preheat the wok on medium-high. Add the vegetable oil and heat until it starts to shimmer.
4. **Cook the Ribs:** Add the marinated ribs to the wok, reserving the marinade. Brown the ribs on all sides, about 5-7 minutes.
5. **Simmer with Sauce:** Pour the marinade that was set aside over the ribs. Turn down the heat to low, cover, and let simmer for 1 hour, stirring occasionally, until the ribs are soft and the sauce is thicker.

Serving:

6. **Garnish and Serve:** Transfer the ribs to a serving dish. Add some sesame seeds and sliced green onions as garnish. Serve immediately with steamed rice or your preferred side dish. Enjoy your Honey Garlic Pork Ribs!

LAMB AND MINT STIR-FRY

Servings: 4

Prep Time: 20 minutes (including marinating time of 10 minutes)

Cook Time: 15 minutes

Total Ingredients: 9

Nutrition Facts (per serving):

Calories: 320 | Fat: 18g | Carbohydrates: 10g | Protein: 25g | Sodium: 450mg | Cholesterol: 70mg

Ingredients:

» 1 lb lamb loin, thinly sliced
» 2 tablespoons soy sauce
» 1 tablespoon cornstarch
» 2 tablespoons vegetable oil, divided
» 1 red bell pepper, thinly sliced
» 1 onion, thinly sliced
» 3 cloves garlic, minced
» 1 tablespoon fresh mint leaves, chopped
» 1 tablespoon hoisin sauce

Preparation:

1. **Marinate the Lamb:** In a bowl, mix the lamb slices with soy sauce and cornstarch. Let it marinate for 10 minutes.
2. **Prepare the Vegetables:** While the lamb is marinating, thinly slice the red bell pepper and onion, and mince the garlic.

Cooking:

3. **Stir-Fry the Lamb:** Heat jup 1 tablespoon of vegetable oil in the wok on high heat. After adding the marinated lamb, stir-fry it for 5-6 minutes, until it is browned and almost done. Take the lamb out of the wok and place it on a dish.
4. **Cook the Vegetables:** Pour the remaining tablespoon of vegetable oil into the wok. Once hot, add the minced garlic and stir-fry for 30 seconds until it releases its aroma. Mix in the bell pepper and onion slices, stir-frying for 2-3 minutes until they are crisp-tender.
5. **Combine Ingredients:** Place the lamb back into the wok and add the chopped mint leaves and hoisin sauce. Mix well and cook for 2-3 more minutes until everything is well mixed and cooked through.

Serving:

6. **Serve Immediately:** Transfer the lamb and mint stir-fry to a serving dish. Serve hot over noodles or steamed rice and enjoy your Lamb and Mint Stir-Fry!

HEARTY BEEF STEW WITH MUSHROOMS

Servings: 4
Prep Time: 15 minutes
Cook Time: 1 hour 30 minutes
Total Ingredients: 10

Nutrition Facts (per serving):
Calories: 400 | Fat: 20g | Carbohydrates: 20g | Protein: 30g | Sodium: 600mg | Cholesterol: 80mg

Ingredients:

» 1.5 lbs beef chuck, diced into into bite-sized pieces
» 2 tablespoons flour
» 2 tablespoons vegetable oil, divided
» 1 onion, chopped
» 3 cloves garlic, minced
» 8 oz mushrooms, sliced
» 2 cups beef broth
» 1 tablespoon soy sauce
» 1 teaspoon thyme
» 1 bay leaf

Preparation:

1. **Dredge the Beef:** In a bowl, toss the beef cubes with flour to coat.
2. **Prepare the Vegetables:** Chop the onion, mince the garlic, and slice the mushrooms.

Cooking:

3. **Brown the Beef:** Set the wok on medium-high heat and add 1 tablespoon of vegetable oil. Add the beef cubes and brown on all sides for 5-7 minutes. Take the beef out of the wok and place on a dish.
4. **Cook the Vegetables:** Pour the second tablespoon of vegetable oil into the wok. Mix in the chopped onion and minced garlic, stir-frying for 2-3 minutes until the onion becomes translucent. Toss the sliced mushrooms and cook for 2-3 minutes until they are soft.
5. **Combine and Simmer:** Bring the beef back into the wok. Combine the beef broth, soy sauce, thyme, and bay leaf. Bring to a boil, then turn down the heat and let it cook slowly, covered, for 1 hour, stirring occasionally, until the beef is tender and the flavors are well combined.

Serving:

6. **Serve the Stew:** Take the bay leaf out before serving. Ladle the beef and mushroom stew into bowls and serve hot with crusty bread or steamed rice. Enjoy your Hearty Beef Stew with Mushrooms!

SLOW-COOKED LAMB SHANK WITH GARLIC AND HERBS

Servings: 4
Prep Time: 15 minutes
Cook Time: 2 hours 30 minutes
Total Ingredients: 10

Nutrition Facts (per serving):
Calories: 480 | Fat: 25g | Carbohydrates: 12g | Protein: 45g | Sodium: 700mg | Cholesterol: 110mg

Ingredients:

- » 4 lamb shanks
- » 2 tablespoons flour
- » 2 tablespoons olive oil
- » 1 onion, chopped
- » 4 cloves garlic, minced
- » 2 cups beef broth
- » 1 cup red wine
- » 1 tablespoon fresh rosemary, chopped
- » 1 tablespoon fresh thyme, chopped
- » Salt and pepper to taste

Preparation:

1. **Dredge the Lamb Shanks:** In a bowl, toss the lamb shanks with flour to coat.
2. **Prepare the Ingredients:** Chop the onion, mince the garlic, and chop the rosemary and thyme.

Cooking:

3. **Brown the Lamb Shanks:** Heat the olive oil in the wok on medium-high. Add the lamb shanks and brown on all sides, about 10 minutes. Take out of the wok and place it aside on a dish.
4. **Cook the Vegetables:** Put the chopped onion and minced garlic to the wok. It will take about 5 minutes of cooking until the onion is clear.
5. **Combine Ingredients:** Return the lamb shanks to the wok. Add the beef broth, red wine, rosemary, thyme, salt, and pepper. Once it reaches a boil, turn down the heat.
6. **Slow Cook:** Put the lid on the wok and cook for two hours, turning the lamb shanks occasionally, till the meat is soft and falls off the bone.

Serving:

7. **Serve the Lamb Shanks:** Transfer the lamb shanks to a platter and pour the sauce on top. It goes well with mashed potatoes or crusty bread. Enjoy your Slow-Cooked Lamb Shank with Garlic and Herbs!

SPICY KOREAN BEEF BOWL

Servings: 4

Prep Time: 20 minutes (including marinating time of 10 minutes)

Cook Time: 15 minutes

Total Ingredients: 9

Nutrition Facts (per serving):
Calories: 420 | Fat: 15g | Carbohydrates: 35g | Protein: 30g | Sodium: 800mg | Cholesterol: 70mg

Ingredients:

- » 1 lb beef sirloin, thinly sliced
- » 2 tablespoons gochujang (Korean red chili paste)
- » 2 tablespoons soy sauce
- » 1 tablespoon sesame oil
- » 2 cloves garlic, minced
- » 1 tablespoon brown sugar
- » 2 cups cooked rice
- » 1 cup shredded carrots
- » 1 cup cucumber, thinly sliced
- » 1 green onion, sliced (for garnish)
- » Sesame seeds (for garnish)

Preparation:

1. **Marinate the Beef:** In a bowl, mix gochujang, soy sauce, sesame oil, minced garlic, and brown sugar. Put the sliced beef in and stir thoroughly. Give it at least ten minutes to marinate.
2. **Prepare the Vegetables:** Shred the carrots and slice the cucumber and green onion.

Cooking:

3. **Heat the Wok:** Preheat the wok on medium-high until it starts to give off a bit of smoke.
4. **Cook the Beef:** Stir-fry the marinated beef in the wok until it is cooked through and caramelized.
5. **Combine Ingredients:** In the last minute of cooking, add the shredded carrots to the wok and stir to combine and heat through.

Serving:

6. **Assemble the Bowl:** Fill four dishes with the cooked rice.. Add the spicy Korean beef and carrots on top and the sliced cucumber on the side.
7. **Garnish and Serve:** Sprinkle with sliced green onions and sesame seeds. Serve immediately and enjoy your Spicy Korean Beef Bowl!

ORANGE-GLAZED CHICKEN THIGHS

Servings: 4

Prep Time: 10 minutes

Cook Time: 20 minutes

Total Ingredients: 8

Nutrition Facts (per serving):
Calories: 340 | Fat: 14g | Carbohydrates: 22g | Protein: 28g | Sodium: 600mg | Cholesterol: 80mg

Ingredients:

» 1 lb chicken thighs, boneless and skinless
» 1/4 cup fresh orange juice
» 2 tablespoons soy sauce
» 2 tablespoons honey
» 1 tablespoon rice vinegar
» 2 cloves garlic, minced
» 1 tablespoon vegetable oil
» 1 teaspoon fresh ginger, grated

Preparation:

1. **Marinate the Chicken:** In a mixing bowl, combine orange juice, soy sauce, honey, rice vinegar, minced garlic, and grated ginger. Add the chicken thighs and let them marinate for at least 10 minutes.
2. **Prepare the Ingredients:** Mince the garlic and grate the ginger if not already done.

Cooking:

3. **Heat the Wok:** Preheat the wok on a medium-high temperature. Add the vegetable oil and heat until it starts to shimmer.
4. **Cook the Chicken:** Place the marinated chicken thighs into the wok. Cook for 15 minutes, turning from time to time, until the chicken is well cooked and caramelized.
5. **Add the Glaze:** Pour any remaining marinade over the chicken in the last 2 minutes of cooking, allowing it to thicken and coat the chicken thighs.

Serving:

6. **Serve the Chicken:** Transfer the orange-glazed chicken thighs to a serving dish. Serve immediately with steamed rice or vegetables. Enjoy your Orange-Glazed Chicken Thighs!

SAVORY DUCK STIR-FRY

Servings: 4

Prep Time: 25 minutes (including marinating time of 10 minutes)

Cook Time: 20 minutes

Total Ingredients: 10

Nutrition Facts (per serving):
Calories: 350 | Fat: 18g | Carbohydrates: 14g | Protein: 30g | Sodium: 700mg | Cholesterol: 80mg

Ingredients:

- » 1 lb duck breast, thinly sliced
- » 2 tablespoons soy sauce
- » 1 tablespoon hoisin sauce
- » 2 tablespoons vegetable oil
- » 1 red bell pepper, sliced
- » 1 yellow bell pepper, sliced
- » 1 cup baby corn, cut into bite-sized pieces
- » 2 cloves garlic, minced
- » 1 tablespoon fresh ginger, grated
- » 2 green onions, sliced

Preparation:

1. **Marinate the Duck:** In a bowl, mix soy sauce and hoisin sauce. Put the duck slices in and let it soak for 10 minutes.
2. **Prepare the Vegetables:** Slice the bell peppers, baby corn, garlic, ginger, and green onions.

Cooking:

3. **Heat the Wok:** Preheat the wok on medium-high. Add 1 tablespoon of vegetable oil.
4. **Cook the Duck:** Add the duck slices to the wok. Stir-fry for 5-7 minutes until browned and well cooked. Lift them from the wok and place them on a dish.
5. **Stir-Fry the Vegetables:** Fill the wok with the rest of the vegetable oil. Add the garlic and ginger, stir-fry for 30 seconds. The baby corn and bell pepper should be added next. Stir-fry for 3-4 minutes to have the vegetables tender-crisp.
6. **Combine and Finish:** Bring the duck back into the wok. Mix well to combine with the vegetables. Continue cooking for another 2 minutes until everything is well done.

Serving:

7. **Serve the Stir-Fry:** Move to a serving dish. Garnish with sliced green onions and serve immediately with steamed rice.

CHICKEN AND BROCCOLI NOODLE BOWL

Servings: 4

Prep Time: 20 minutes (including marinating time of 10 minutes)

Cook Time: 15 minutes

Total Ingredients: 9

Nutrition Facts (per serving):

Calories: 320 | Fat: 8g | Carbohydrates: 40g | Protein: 22g | Sodium: 600mg | Cholesterol: 50mg

Ingredients:

» 1 lb chicken breast, thinly sliced
» 1 tablespoon soy sauce
» 2 tablespoons oyster sauce
» 2 tablespoons vegetable oil
» 2 cups broccoli florets
» 3 cloves garlic, minced
» 1 tablespoon fresh ginger, grated
» 8 oz rice noodles
» 2 green onions, sliced

Preparation:

1. **Marinate the Chicken:** In a bowl, mix soy sauce and oyster sauce. Add the chicken slices and marinate for 10 minutes.
2. **Prepare the Ingredients:** Mince the garlic and ginger, slice the green onions, and cut the broccoli into florets. Follow the directions on the package to cook the rice noodles, then drain them.

Cooking:

3. **Heat the Wok:** Preheat the wok over medium-high heat. Put in 1 tablespoon of vegetable oil.
4. **Cook the Chicken:** Add the chicken to the wok. Stir-fry for 5-7 minutes until browned and cooked through. Remove from the wok and set aside.
5. **Stir-Fry the Vegetables:** Add the second tablespoon of vegetable oil to the wok. Mix in the garlic and ginger, stir-fry for 30 seconds, then put in the broccoli florets. Stir-fry for 3-4 minutes until they are soft.
6. **Combine and Finish:** Place the chicken back into the wok. Add the cooked rice noodles. Stir well to combine with the vegetables. Cook for 2-3 more minutes until all ingredients are fully heated.

Serving:

7. **Serve the Noodle Bowl:** Transfer to bowls. Garnish with sliced green onions and serve immediately.

SPICY SZECHUAN CHICKEN

Servings: 4

Prep Time: 20 minutes (including marinating time of 10 minutes)

Cook Time: 15 minutes

Total Ingredients: 8

Nutrition Facts (per serving):

Calories: 300 | Fat: 10g | Carbohydrates: 20g | Protein: 28g | Sodium: 700mg | Cholesterol: 75mg

Ingredients:

- » 1 lb chicken breast, thinly sliced
- » 2 tablespoons soy sauce
- » 1 tablespoon rice vinegar
- » 2 tablespoons vegetable oil
- » 3 cloves garlic, minced
- » 1 tablespoon Szechuan peppercorns
- » 1 red bell pepper, thinly sliced
- » 1 tablespoon chili paste

Preparation:

1. **Marinate the Chicken:** In a bowl, mix soy sauce and rice vinegar. Add the chicken slices and marinate for 10 minutes.
2. **Prepare the Ingredients:** Mince the garlic, slice the red bell pepper.

Cooking:

3. **Heat the Wok:** Preheat the wok over medium-high heat. Add 1 tablespoon of vegetable oil.
4. **Cook the Chicken:** Add the chicken to the wok. Stir-fry for 5-7 minutes until browned and cooked through. Take out of the wok and place on a dish.
5. **Stir-Fry the Vegetables:** Pour the second tablespoon of vegetable oil into the wok. Mix in the minced garlic and Szechuan peppercorns, stir-fry for 30 seconds. Add the red bell pepper and stir-fry for 2-3 minutes.
6. **Combine and Finish:** Place the chicken back into the wok. Add the chili paste. Stir well to combine with the vegetables. Last step is cooking for 2-3 additional minutes until all ingredients are fully heated through.

Serving:

7. **Serve the Dish:** Place on a serving dish, with steamed rice. Enjoy your Spicy Szechuan Chicken!

DUCK AND RICE SOUP

Servings: 4

Prep Time: 15 minutes

Cook Time: 1 hour 30 minutes

Total Ingredients: 9

Nutrition Facts (per serving):

Calories: 380 | Fat: 18g | Carbohydrates: 24g | Protein: 28g | Sodium: 600mg | Cholesterol: 90mg

Ingredients:

- » 1 lb duck breast, sliced
- » 1 cup jasmine rice
- » 6 cups chicken broth
- » 1 onion, chopped
- » 2 cloves garlic, minced
- » 1 tablespoon ginger, grated
- » 1 tablespoon soy sauce
- » 2 green onions, sliced
- » 1 tablespoon sesame oil

Preparation:

1. **Prepare the Duck:** Slice the duck breast into thin pieces.
2. **Chop the Vegetables:** Chop the onion, mince the garlic, grate the ginger, and slice the green onions.

Cooking:

3. **Heat the Wok:** Preheat the wok on medium heat. Add the sesame oil.
4. **Cook the Duck:** Place the duck slices into the wok. Stir-fry for 5-7 minutes, until cooked through and golden. Take off the wok and move onto a plate.
5. **Cook the Aromatics:** In the same wok, toss in the chopped onion, minced garlic, and grated ginger. Stir-fry for 2-3 minutes until fragrant.
6. **Add the Broth and Rice:** Pour in the chicken broth and soy sauce. Heat up to boil, then add the jasmine rice. Reduce the heat and simmer for about 20 minutes, or until the rice is cooked.
7. **Add the Duck:** Bring the duck back into the wok. Simmer for a further 10 minutes to let flavors combine.

Serving:

8. **Serve the Soup:** Spoon the soup into bowls. Garnish with sliced green onions and serve hot.

FIVE-SPICE DUCK BREAST

Servings: 4

Prep Time: 40 minutes (including marinating time of 30 minutes)

Cook Time: 20 minutes

Total Ingredients: 7

Nutrition Facts (per serving):
Calories: 350 | Fat: 18g | Carbohydrates: 4g | Protein: 40g | Sodium: 450mg | Cholesterol: 120mg

Ingredients:

- » 4 duck breasts, skin on
- » 2 tablespoons soy sauce
- » 1 tablespoon hoisin sauce
- » 1 tablespoon honey
- » 1 teaspoon Chinese five-spice powder
- » 2 cloves garlic, minced
- » 1 tablespoon vegetable oil

Preparation:

1. **Prepare the Duck Marinade:** In a bowl, combine soy sauce, hoisin sauce, honey, Chinese five-spice powder, and minced garlic.
2. **Marinate the Duck:** Make shallow cuts in the skin of the duck breasts in a crisscross pattern. Put the duck breasts to soak and let them sit for 30 minutes.

Cooking:

3. **Heat the Wok:** Preheat the wok on medium-high heat. Add vegetable oil.
4. **Cook the Duck:** Position the duck breasts in the wok, skin side down. Cook for 6-8 minutes until the skin is crispy. Turn and cook for another 6-8 minutes until the duck is cooked to your desired doneness.
5. **Rest the Duck:** Lift the duck from the wok and allow it to rest for 5 minutes.

Serving:

6. **Slice and Serve:** Slice the duck breasts thinly. Serve with steamed rice and your favorite vegetables. Enjoy your Five-Spice Duck Breast!

ZESTY PINEAPPLE CHICKEN BITES

Servings: 4
Prep Time: 15 minutes
Cook Time: 15 minutes
Total Ingredients: 10

Nutrition Facts (per serving):
Calories: 300 | Fat: 12g | Carbohydrates: 25g | Protein: 25g | Sodium: 600mg | Cholesterol: 70mg

Ingredients:

» 1 lb chicken breast, cut into small pieces
» 1/2 cup cornstarch
» 1 egg, beaten
» 2 tablespoons vegetable oil
» 1/2 cup pineapple chunks
» 1 red bell pepper, diced
» 1/2 cup sweet and sour sauce
» 1 tablespoon soy sauce
» 1 tablespoon rice vinegar
» 2 green onions, sliced

Preparation:

1. **Prepare the Chicken:** Cut the chicken breast into small pieces. Toss the chicken pieces in cornstarch and dip them in the beaten egg.
2. **Prepare the Vegetables:** Chop the red bell pepper and slice the green onions.

Cooking:

3. **Heat the Wok:** Preheat the wok over medium-high heat. Add vegetable oil.
4. **Cook the Chicken:** Put the chicken pieces into the wok and stir-fry until golden brown and crispy, for 5-7 minutes. Take the chicken out and place it on a dish.
5. **Cook the Vegetables:** Add the chopped pepper and pineapple chunks to the wok. Stir-fry for 2-3 minutes.
6. **Add the Sauce:** In a bowl, mix sweet and sour sauce, soy sauce, and rice vinegar. Transfer the sauce into the wok and heat it until it simmers.
7. **Combine:** Return the chicken to the wok and stir well to coat with the sauce. Cook for 2-3 additional minutes until all ingredients are cooked through.

Serving:

8. **Garnish and Serve:** Place the chicken on a serving dish. Sprinkle some sliced green onions. Serve immediately with noodles or steamed rice. Enjoy your Zesty Pineapple Chicken Bites!

FLAVORFUL SHRIMP RICE BOWL

Servings: 4
Prep Time: 10 minutes
Cook Time: 30 minutes
Total Ingredients: 9

Nutrition Facts (per serving):
Calories: 350 | Fat: 10g | Carbohydrates: 45g | Protein: 20g | Sodium: 700mg | Cholesterol: 130mg

Ingredients:

» 1 lb medium shrimp, peeled and deveined
» 1 1/2 cups uncooked rice
» 3 cups water
» 2 tablespoons vegetable oil
» 2 eggs, beaten
» 1 cup frozen peas and carrots, thawed
» 3 green onions, sliced
» 3 tablespoons soy sauce
» 1 tablespoon oyster sauce
» 1 teaspoon sesame oil

Preparation:

1. **Cook the Rice:** In a medium pot, bring 3 cups of water to a boil. Add the uncooked rice, reduce the heat to low, cover, and simmer for about 15 minutes, or until the water is absorbed and the rice is cooked. Let it cool slightly before using.
2. **Prepare the Ingredients:** Thaw the frozen peas and carrots, slice the green onions, and ensure the shrimp are peeled and deveined.

Cooking:

3. **Heat the Wok:** Preheat the wok over medium-high heat. Add 1 tablespoon of vegetable oil.
4. **Cook the Shrimp:** Add the shrimp to the wok and stir-fry until they turn pink and are cooked through, for 2-3 minutes. Remove the shrimp and set aside.
5. **Cook the Eggs:** Add the beaten eggs to the wok and scramble until they are cooked through. Remove and set aside with the shrimp.
6. **Cook the Vegetables:** Pour the second tablespoon of vegetable oil into the wok. Add the peas and carrots and stir-fry for 2 minutes.
7. **Add the Rice:** Transfer the cooked rice to the wok, breaking up any clumps with a spatula. Stir-fry for 3-4 minutes until the rice is hot.
8. **Combine Ingredients:** Bring the cooked shrimp and eggs back into the wok. Add the sliced green onions, soy sauce, oyster sauce, and sesame oil. Stir well to combine and cook for another 2 minutes.

Serving:

9. **Serve the Dish:** Place the Flavorful Shrimp Rice into 4 bowls. Serve immediately, garnished with additional green onions if desired. Enjoy your Flavorful Shrimp Rice Bowl!

BEEF CHOW FUN

Servings: 4
Prep Time: 15 minutes
Cook Time: 15 minutes
Total Ingredients: 10

Nutrition Facts (per serving):
Calories: 400 | Fat: 14g | Carbohydrates: 50g | Protein: 20g | Sodium: 850mg | Cholesterol: 40mg

Ingredients:
» 1 lb beef sirloin, thinly sliced
» 1 lb wide rice noodles, soaked or boiled as per package instructions
» 3 tablespoons soy sauce
» 2 tablespoons oyster sauce
» 1 tablespoon dark soy sauce
» 2 tablespoons vegetable oil
» 1 medium onion, sliced
» 2 cloves garlic, minced
» 1 cup bean sprouts
» 3 green onions, cut into 2-inch lengths

Preparation:
1. **Prepare the Beef:** Thinly slice the beef sirloin against the grain.
2. **Prepare the Noodles:** Soak or boil the wide rice noodles as directed on the box, until they are firm but still soft. Drain and place on a dish.

Cooking:
3. **Heat the Wok:** Preheat the wok over high heat. Add 1 tablespoon of vegetable oil.
4. **Cook the Beef:** Add the beef to the wok and stir-fry until it is browned and cooked through, about 3-4 minutes. Take out and place aside.
5. **Cook the Vegetables:** Add the remaining tablespoon of vegetable oil to the wok. Add the sliced onion and garlic, and stir-fry for 2 minutes until the onion is tender.
6. **Add the Noodles:** Add the soaked or boiled rice noodles to the wok. Stir-fry for 3-4 minutes, ensuring the noodles are well-separated and coated in oil.
7. **Combine Ingredients:** Place the cooked beef back into the wok. Add the bean sprouts and green onions. Stir in the soy sauce, oyster sauce, and dark soy sauce. Mix well and stir-fry for another 2-3 minutes until everything is hot and well combined.

Serving:
8. **Serve the Dish:** Transfer the Beef Chow Fun to a serving platter. Serve immediately and enjoy the savory and satisfying flavors of this classic dish!

VEGETABLE LO MEIN

Servings: 4
Prep Time: 10 minutes
Cook Time: 15 minutes
Total Ingredients: 10

Nutrition Facts (per serving):
Calories: 320 | Fat: 8g | Carbohydrates: 50g | Protein: 10g | Sodium: 750mg | Cholesterol: 0mg

Ingredients:

» 8 oz lo mein noodles
» 2 tablespoons vegetable oil
» 1 medium onion, thinly sliced
» 2 cloves garlic, minced
» 1 cup bell peppers, julienned
» 1 cup broccoli florets
» 1 carrot, julienned
» 1/4 cup soy sauce
» 1 tablespoon oyster sauce
» 1 teaspoon sesame oil

Preparation:

1. **Prepare the Noodles:** Follow the directions on the package to cook the lo mein noodles. Drain and keep aside.
2. **Prepare the Vegetables:** Thinly slice the onion and julienne the bell peppers and carrots. Separate the broccoli into small florets.

Cooking:

3. **Heat the Wok:** Preheat the wok over medium-high heat. Add 1 tablespoon of vegetable oil.
4. **Stir-Fry the Aromatics:** Add the sliced onion and minced garlic to the wok. Stir-fry for 2 minutes until aromatic and the onion is clear.
5. **Add the Vegetables:** Add the bell peppers, broccoli, and carrots to the wok. Stir-fry for 5-7 minutes.
6. **Combine Noodles and Sauce:** Add the cooked noodles to the wok. Pour in the soy sauce, oyster sauce, and sesame oil. Mix well and heat through, about 2-3 minutes.

Serving:

7. **Serve the Dish:** Place the Vegetable Lo Mein to a serving dish. Serve immediately and enjoy a nutritious and flavorful meal!

GOLDEN CHICKEN RICE FEAST

Servings: 4
Prep Time: 25 minutes
Cook Time: 15 minutes
Total Ingredients: 10

Nutrition Facts (per serving):
Calories: 370 | Fat: 12g | Carbohydrates: 45g | Protein: 20g | Sodium: 800mg | Cholesterol: 70mg

Ingredients:

» 1 lb boneless, skinless chicken breast, diced
» 1 1/2 cups uncooked rice (to make 3 cups cooked rice)
» 3 cups water
» 2 tablespoons vegetable oil
» 2 eggs, beaten
» 1 cup frozen peas and carrots, thawed
» 3 green onions, sliced
» 3 tablespoons soy sauce
» 1 tablespoon oyster sauce
» 1 teaspoon sesame oil

Preparation:

1. **Cook the Rice:** In a medium saucepan, bring 3 cups of water to a boil. Add 1 1/2 cups of rice, reduce the heat to low, cover, and simmer for about 15 minutes or until the rice is tender and water is absorbed. Fluff with a fork and let cool slightly.
2. **Prepare the Chicken:** Dice the chicken breast into small pieces.
3. **Prepare the Vegetables:** Thaw the frozen peas and carrots. Slice the green onions.

Cooking:

4. **Heat the Wok:** Preheat the wok over medium-high heat. Add 1 tablespoon of vegetable oil.
5. **Cook the Chicken:** Add the diced chicken to the wok and stir-fry until fully cooked, about 5-7 minutes. Take off the wok and place aside on a dish.
6. **Cook the Eggs:** Add the beaten eggs to the wok and scramble until fully cooked. Remove and place on a dish with the chicken.
7. **Cook the Vegetables:** Pour the second tablespoon of vegetable oil into the wok. Add the peas and carrots, and stir-fry for 2 minutes.
8. **Add the Rice:** Transfer the cooked rice to the wok, breaking up any clumps with a spatula. Stir-fry for 3-4 minutes until the rice is hot.
9. **Combine Ingredients:** Return the cooked chicken and eggs to the wok. Add the sliced green onions, soy sauce, oyster sauce, and sesame oil. Mix well and cook for 2-3 minutes until everything is fully heated.

Serving:

10. **Serve the Dish:** Place the Golden Chicken Rice Feast onto a serving platter. Serve immediately and enjoy a satisfying and flavorful meal!

SPICY THAI NOODLES

Servings: 4
Prep Time: 10 minutes
Cook Time: 15 minutes
Total Ingredients: 9

Nutrition Facts (per serving):
Calories: 350 | Fat: 10g | Carbohydrates: 50g | Protein: 10g | Sodium: 600mg | Cholesterol: 0mg

Ingredients:

- » 8 oz rice noodles
- » 2 tablespoons vegetable oil
- » 1 red bell pepper, thinly sliced
- » 2 cloves garlic, minced
- » 1 cup bean sprouts
- » 1/4 cup chopped peanuts
- » 2 tablespoons soy sauce
- » 2 tablespoons sriracha sauce
- » 2 green onions, sliced

Preparation:

1. **Prepare the Noodles:** Follow the directions on the package to cook the rice noodles. Drain and place aside.
2. **Prepare the Vegetables:** Thinly slice the red bell pepper, mince the garlic, and slice the green onions.

Cooking:

3. **Heat the Wok:** Preheat the wok on medium-high. Add the vegetable oil.
4. **Stir-Fry the Aromatics:** Put the minced garlic into the wok and stir-fry for 30 seconds until aromatic.
5. **Add the Vegetables:** Add the red bell pepper and stir-fry for 3-4 minutes until tender-crisp.
6. **Mix the Noodles with the Sauce:** Add the cooked rice noodles to the wok. Pour in the soy sauce and sriracha sauce. Stir well to combine and heat through, about 2-3 minutes.
7. **Add Bean Sprouts:** Toss in the bean sprouts and stir-fry for another minute.

Serving:

8. **Serve the Dish:** Transfer the Spicy Thai Noodles to a platter. Sprinkle with chopped peanuts and sliced green onions. Serve right away and enjoy the spicy, tangy flavors!

KIMCHI RICE SIZZLE

Servings: 4
Prep Time: 5 minutes
Cook Time: 20 minutes
Total Ingredients: 8

Nutrition Facts (per serving):
Calories: 400 | Fat: 12g | Carbohydrates: 55g | Protein: 15g | Sodium: 800mg | Cholesterol: 50mg

Ingredients:
» 1 cup uncooked jasmine rice
» 2 cups water
» 1 cup kimchi, chopped
» 2 tablespoons kimchi juice
» 2 tablespoons vegetable oil
» 2 eggs, beaten
» 2 green onions, cut into 2-inch segments
» 1 tablespoon soy sauce
» 1 teaspoon gochujang (Korean chili paste)

Preparation:
1. **Cook the Rice:** In a medium pot, combine the uncooked jasmine rice and water. Bring to a boil, then reduce the heat to low, cover, and simmer for 15 minutes or until the water is absorbed and the rice is tender. Fluff with a fork and set aside.
2. **Prepare the Kimchi:** While the rice is cooking, chop the kimchi and set aside. Slice the green onions.

Cooking:
3. **Heat the Wok:** Preheat the wok over medium-high heat. Add the vegetable oil.
4. **Cook the Eggs:** Add the beaten eggs to the wok and scramble until fully cooked. Remove and set aside.
5. **Cook the Kimchi:** Add the chopped kimchi to the wok and stir-fry for 2-3 minutes until heated through and fragrant.
6. **Add the Rice:** Transfer the cooked rice to the wok, using a spatula to break up any clumps. Stir-fry for 3-4 minutes until the rice is thoroughly heated.
7. **Combine Ingredients:** Return the scrambled eggs to the wok. Add the kimchi juice, soy sauce, and gochujang. Mix well and cook for another 2-3 minutes.

Serving:
8. **Serve the Dish:** Transfer the Kimchi Rice Sizzle to a platter. Garnish with sliced green onions. Serve immediately and enjoy the spicy, tangy flavors!

SINGAPORE NOODLES

Servings: 4
Prep Time: 10 minutes
Cook Time: 15 minutes
Total Ingredients: 9

Nutrition Facts (per serving):
Calories: 320 | Fat: 8g | Carbohydrates: 50g | Protein: 20g | Sodium: 700mg | Cholesterol: 100mg

Ingredients:

» 8 oz rice vermicelli noodles
» 2 tablespoons vegetable oil
» 1 small onion, thinly sliced
» 1 red bell pepper, thinly sliced
» 1 cup shredded cabbage
» 1/2 cup cooked shrimp or chicken, sliced
» 1 tablespoon curry powder
» 2 tablespoons soy sauce
» 2 green onions, sliced

Preparation:

1. **Prepare the Noodles:** Prepare the rice vermicelli noodles following the directions on the package. Once cooked, drain them and put them aside.
» **Prepare the Vegetables:** Thinly slice the onion and red bell pepper, shred the cabbage, and slice the green onions.

Cooking:

2. **Heat the Wok:** Preheat the wok over medium-high heat. Add the vegetable oil.
3. **Stir-Fry the Aromatics:** Place the sliced onion into the wok and stir-fry for 2 minutes until softened.
4. **Add the Vegetables:** Add the red bell pepper and shredded cabbage. Stir-fry for 3-4 minutes until tender-crisp.
5. **Add the Protein and Curry:** Add the cooked shrimp or chicken to the wok. Sprinkle the curry powder over the mixture and stir well to combine.
6. **Mix the Noodles with the Sauce:** Add the cooked noodles to the wok. Pour in the soy sauce and stir well to coat the noodles and combine all ingredients. Cook for 2-3 more minutes until everything is heated through.

Serving:

7. **Serve the Dish:** Transfer the Singapore Noodles to a serving dish. Garnish with sliced green onions. Serve immediately and enjoy the vibrant, curry-infused flavors!

SAVORY TOFU VEGETABLE FUSION

Servings: 4
Prep Time: 10 minutes
Cook Time: 10 minutes
Total Ingredients: 9

Nutrition Facts (per serving):
Calories: 250 | Fat: 12g | Carbohydrates: 18g | Protein: 15g | Sodium: 500mg | Cholesterol: 0mg

Ingredients:

» 1 block (14 oz) firm tofu, drained and cubed
» 2 tablespoons vegetable oil, divided
» 1 cup snap peas
» 1 cup mushrooms, sliced
» 1 red bell pepper, thinly sliced
» 2 cloves garlic, minced
» 2 tablespoons soy sauce
» 1 tablespoon sriracha sauce
» 1 teaspoon sesame oil

Preparation:

1. **Prepare the Tofu:** Drain and cube the tofu. Slice the red bell pepper and mushrooms. Trim the snap peas. Mince the garlic.

Cooking:

2. **Crisp the Tofu:** Heat 1 tablespoon of vegetable oil in the wok over medium-high heat. Add the cubed tofu and stir-fry until golden and crispy, about 5-7 minutes. Remove from the wok and set aside.

3. **Stir-Fry the Vegetables:** Add the last tablespoon of vegetable oil to the wok. Put the garlic in and stir-fry for 30 seconds until aromatic. Add the snap peas, mushrooms, and red bell pepper. Sauté for 3-4 minutes until they reach a tender-crisp texture.

4. **Mix the Tofu with the Sauce:** Bring the tofu back into the wok. Add the soy sauce, sriracha sauce, and sesame oil. Stir well to coat all the ingredients and cook for 2-3 more minutes to combine everything and ensure they are thoroughly heated.

Serving:

5. **Serve:** Transfer the Savory Tofu Vegetable Fusion to a platter. Serve immediately with steamed rice or your favorite side dish. Enjoy the spicy, flavorful goodness!

CRISPY VEGETABLE EGG ROLLS

Servings: 4 (makes about 12 egg rolls)

Prep Time: 15 minutes

Cook Time: 10 minutes

Total Ingredients: 9

Nutrition Facts (per serving):
Calories: 200 | Fat: 10g | Carbohydrates: 25g | Protein: 4g | Sodium: 400mg | Cholesterol: 0mg

Ingredients:

»   1 cup shredded cabbage
»   1 cup shredded carrots
»   1/2 cup bean sprouts
»   2 green onions, finely chopped
»   2 cloves garlic, minced
»   1 tablespoon soy sauce
»   1 teaspoon sesame oil
»   12 egg roll wrappers
»   Vegetable oil for frying

Preparation:

1. **Create the Filling:** In a large mixing bowl, combine shredded cabbage, shredded carrots, bean sprouts, and chopped green onions. Mix in the minced garlic, soy sauce, and sesame oil. Stir well.
2. **Wrap the Egg Rolls:** Place an egg roll wrapper on a clean surface. Spoon about 2 tablespoons of the vegetable mixture into the center. Fold the bottom corner over the filling, tuck in the sides, and roll up tightly. Dab a little water on the edge to seal it. Repeat this process with the remaining wrappers and filling.

Cooking:

3. **Heat the Oil:** Heat about 2 inches of vegetable oil in a wok over medium-high heat until it reaches 350°F.
4. **Fry the Egg Rolls:** Carefully add the egg rolls to the hot oil, a few at a time, and fry until golden brown and crispy, about 3-4 minutes. Use a slotted spoon to lift them out of the oil and place them on paper towels to drain.

Serving:

5. **Serve the Dish:** Serve the Crispy Vegetable Egg Rolls hot with your favorite dipping condiment, such as soy sauce or sweet chili sauce. Enjoy the crunchy, savory treat!

GARLIC GREEN BEANS

Servings: 4

Prep Time: 5 minutes

Cook Time: 10 minutes

Total Ingredients: 6

Nutrition Facts (per serving): Calories: 90 | Fat: 4g | Carbohydrates: 12g | Protein: 3g | Sodium: 300mg | Cholesterol: 0mg

Ingredients:

» 1 lb fresh green beans, trimmed
» 2 tablespoons vegetable oil
» 4 cloves garlic, minced
» 1 tablespoon soy sauce
» 1 teaspoon sesame oil
» Salt and pepper to taste

Preparation:

1. **Prepare the Beans:** Trim the ends of the green beans and rinse them thoroughly.

Cooking:

2. **Heat the Wok:** Preheat the wok over medium-high heat and let it smoke a little.
3. **Stir-Fry the Green Beans:** Add the vegetable oil to the wok. Mix in the green beans and stir-fry for 5-7 minutes until they start to blister and become tender-crisp.
4. **Add the Garlic:** Add the minced garlic to the wok and stir-fry for 1-2 more minutes until the garlic is fragrant and golden brown.
5. **Season:** Pour over the green beans the sesame oil and soy sauce. Toss to coat evenly. Add salt and pepper to taste.

Serving:

6. **Serve the Dish:** Transfer the Garlic Green Beans to a platter. Serve immediately as a side dish to complement your main course. Enjoy the fresh, garlicky flavor!

TOFU AND BOK CHOY STIR-FRY

Servings: 4
Prep Time: 10 minutes
Cook Time: 10 minutes
Total Ingredients: 8

Nutrition Facts (per serving):
Calories: 180 | Fat: 9g | Carbohydrates: 12g | Protein: 15g | Sodium: 400mg | Cholesterol: 0mg

Ingredients:

» 1 block (14 oz) firm tofu, drained and cubed
» 2 tablespoons vegetable oil, divided
» 3 cloves garlic, minced
» 1-inch piece ginger, minced
» 1 lb baby bok choy, halved
» 2 tablespoons soy sauce
» 1 tablespoon oyster sauce
» 1 teaspoon sesame oil

Preparation:

1. **Prepare the Tofu and Bok Choy:** Drain and cube the tofu. Halve the baby bok choy lengthwise. Mince the garlic and ginger.

Cooking:

2. **Crisp the Tofu:** Heat 1 tablespoon of vegetable oil in the wok over medium-high heat. Add the tofu and stir-fry until golden and crispy, about 5-7 minutes. Remove from the wok and set aside.
3. **Stir-Fry the Aromatics:** Fill the wok with the last tablespoon of vegetable oil. Add and stir-fry the ginger and minced garlic for approximately a minute until they release their aroma.
4. **Add the Bok Choy:** Add the halved baby bok choy to the wok and stir-fry for 3-4 minutes until tender-crisp.
5. **Combine and Sauce:** Return the tofu to the wok. Add the soy sauce, oyster sauce, and sesame oil. Toss to coat all the ingredients evenly and cook for 2 more minutes until everything is blended and well hot.

Serving:

6. **Serve the Dish:** Transfer the Tofu and Bok Choy Stir-Fry to a serving dish. Serve with steamed rice or noodles for a complete meal. Enjoy the harmonious blend of flavors and textures!

SESAME SPINACH STIR-FRY

Servings: 4
Prep Time: 5 minutes
Cook Time: 5 minutes
Total Ingredients: 6

Nutrition Facts (per serving): Calories: 70 | Fat: 5g | Carbohydrates: 4g | Protein: 2g | Sodium: 300mg | Cholesterol: 0mg

Ingredients:

» 1 lb fresh spinach, washed and trimmed
» 1 tablespoon vegetable oil
» 3 cloves garlic, minced
» 1 tablespoon soy sauce
» 1 teaspoon sesame oil
» 1 tablespoon sesame seeds, toasted

Preparation:

1. **Prepare the Spinach:** Wash and trim the spinach. Mince the garlic.

Cooking:

2. **Heat the Wok:** Preheat the wok on medium-high until it starts to give off a bit of smoke.
3. **Stir-Fry the Garlic:** Add the vegetable oil to the wok. Put the minced garlic in and stir-fry for about 30 seconds until aromatic.
4. **Add the Spinach:** Add the spinach to the wok and stir-fry for 2-3 minutes until wilted.
5. **Season:** Sprinkle the soy sauce and sesame oil over the spinach. Toss to coat evenly. Sprinkle with toasted sesame seeds.

Serving:

6. **Serve the Dish:** Transfer the Sesame Spinach Stir-Fry to a serving plate. Serve immediately as a side dish to complement your meal. Enjoy the fresh and nutty flavor!

COCONUT CURRY TOFU HARMONY

Servings: 4
Prep Time: 10 minutes
Cook Time: 15 minutes
Total Ingredients: 10

Nutrition Facts (per serving):
Calories: 280 | Fat: 18g | Carbohydrates: 20g | Protein: 10g | Sodium: 500mg | Cholesterol: 0mg

Ingredients:

» 1 block (14 oz) firm tofu, drained and cubed
» 2 tablespoons vegetable oil
» 1 onion, sliced
» 1 bell pepper, sliced
» 1 zucchini, sliced
» 1 cup coconut milk
» 2 tablespoons red curry paste
» 1 tablespoon soy sauce
» 1 teaspoon sugar
» Fresh basil leaves for garnish

Preparation:

1. **Prepare the Tofu and Vegetables:** Drain and cube the tofu. Slice the onion, bell pepper, and zucchini.

Cooking:

2. **Cook the Tofu:** Heat the vegetable oil in the wok over medium-high heat. Add the tofu cubes and stir-fry until golden and crispy, about 5-7 minutes. Lift out of the wok and place on a dish.
3. **Stir-Fry the Vegetables:** In the same wok, add the sliced onion, bell pepper, and zucchini. Stir-fry for 3-4 minutes until the vegetables are soft and crisp.
4. **Add the Sauce:** Add the coconut milk, red curry paste, soy sauce, and sugar to the wok. Stir well to combine and heat until it begins to boil.
5. **Combine and Heat Through:** Return the tofu to the wok. Stir to coat the tofu and vegetables with the curry sauce. Simmer for 2-3 more minutes until all ingredients are well blended and cooked through.

Serving:

6. **Serve the Dish:** Transfer the Coconut Curry Tofu Harmony to a serving bowl. Use fresh basil leaves as garnish. Serve immediately with steamed rice. Enjoy the rich and creamy flavors of this Thai-inspired dish!

TERIYAKI MUSHROOM AND SNOW PEAS

Servings: 4
Prep Time: 5 minutes
Cook Time: 10 minutes
Total Ingredients: 8

Nutrition Facts (per serving):
Calories: 120 | Fat: 5g | Carbohydrates: 15g | Protein: 4g | Sodium: 600mg | Cholesterol: 0mg

Ingredients:

» 2 tablespoons vegetable oil
» 2 cups mushrooms, sliced
» 2 cups snow peas, trimmed
» 3 cloves garlic, minced
» 1/4 cup soy sauce
» 2 tablespoons mirin
» 1 tablespoon sugar
» 1 tablespoon cornstarch mixed with 2 tablespoons water

Preparation:

1. **Prepare the Ingredients:** Slice the mushrooms and trim the snow peas. Mince the garlic.

Cooking:

2. **Heat the Wok:** Preheat the wok over medium-high heat and let it smoke a little.
3. **Stir-Fry the Mushrooms:** Pour the vegetable oil to the wok. Add the sliced mushrooms and stir-fry for 3-4 minutes until they start to golden and soften.
4. **Add the Snow Peas:** Add the snow peas and minced garlic to the wok. Stir-fry for another 2-3 minutes until the snow peas are tender-crisp.
5. **Make the Sauce:** In a small bowl, blend the soy sauce, mirin, and sugar. Transfer the sauce over the vegetables in the wok.
6. **Thicken the Sauce:** Incorporate the cornstarch mixture into the wok and stir thoroughly. Continue cooking for 1-2 more minutes until the sauce thickens and evenly coats the vegetables.

Serving:

7. **Serve the Dish:** Transfer the Teriyaki Mushroom and Snow Peas to a serving platter. Serve with steamed rice or noodles. Enjoy the savory and satisfying taste of this easy stir-fry!

FIERY GARLIC SHRIMP FEAST

Servings: 4
Prep Time: 10 minutes
Cook Time: 10 minutes
Total Ingredients: 8

Nutrition Facts (per serving):
Calories: 210 | Fat: 9g | Carbohydrates: 7g | Protein: 24g | Sodium: 760mg | Cholesterol: 190mg

Ingredients:

» 1 lb shrimp, peeled and deveined
» 2 tablespoons vegetable oil
» 4 cloves garlic, minced
» 1 red bell pepper, sliced
» 1 cup snow peas
» 2 tablespoons soy sauce
» 1 tablespoon sriracha sauce
» 2 green onions, sliced (for garnish)

Preparation:

1. **Prepare the Shrimp and Vegetables:** Peel and devein the shrimp. Slice the red bell pepper and trim the snow peas. Mince the garlic.

Cooking:

2. **Heat the Wok:** Preheat the wok on medium-high until it starts to give off a bit of smoke.
3. **Cook the Shrimp:** Add 1 tablespoon of vegetable oil to the wok. Add the shrimp and stir-fry for 2-3 minutes until they turn pink and are cooked through. Lift from the wok and place aside.
4. **Cook the Vegetables:** Add the second tablespoon of vegetable oil to the wok. Add the minced garlic and stir-fry for 30 seconds until aromatic. Add the red bell pepper and snow peas, and stir-fry for 3-4 minutes until they are soft and crisp.
5. **Combine and Add Sauce:** Return the shrimp to the wok. Add the soy sauce and sriracha sauce. Stir well to cover all ingredients with the sauce. Cook for another 1-2 minutes until everything is heated through.

Serving:

6. **Serve the Dish:** Transfer the Fiery Garlic Shrimp Feast to a platter. Place the sliced green onions as garnish. Serve immediately with steamed rice or noodles. Enjoy the spicy and flavorful taste of this quick stir-fry!

SWEET AND SOUR FISH FILLETS

Servings: 4
Prep Time: 15 minutes
Cook Time: 15 minutes
Total Ingredients: 10

Nutrition Facts (per serving):
Calories: 270 | Fat: 10g | Carbohydrates: 25g | Protein: 20g | Sodium: 600mg | Cholesterol: 55mg

Ingredients:

- 1 lb white fish fillets (such as tilapia or haddock), cut into small pieces
- 1/2 cup cornstarch
- 2 tablespoons vegetable oil
- 1 red bell pepper, diced
- 1 green bell pepper, diced
- 1 cup pineapple chunks
- 1/4 cup rice vinegar
- 2 tablespoons soy sauce
- 2 tablespoons ketchup
- 2 tablespoons brown sugar

Preparation:

1. **Prepare the Fish and Vegetables:** Cut the fish fillets into small pieces. Dice the red and green bell peppers. Drain the pineapple chunks if using canned.

Cooking:

2. **Coat and Fry the Fish:** Dredge the fish pieces in cornstarch, shaking off any excess. Heat the vegetable oil in the wok on medium-high. Add the fish pieces and fry until golden brown and crispy, about 3-4 minutes per side. Take out the fish and place it on a dish.
3. **Stir-Fry the Vegetables:** Add the diced bell peppers to the wok and stir-fry for 2-3 minutes until tender-crisp. Add the pineapple chunks and stir-fry for another minute.
4. **Make the Sauce:** In a small bowl, combine the rice vinegar, soy sauce, ketchup, and brown sugar. Pour the sauce into the wok with the vegetables and bring to a simmer.
5. **Combine and Finish:** Return the fried fish to the wok and gently stir in the sauce to coat. Cook for 2-3 more minutes until all ingredients are well heated and combined.

Serving:

6. **Serve the Dish:** Transfer the Sweet and Sour Fish Fillets to a serving plate. Serve with steamed rice. Enjoy the sweet and tangy flavors of this delightful dish!

LEMON BUTTER SCALLOPS

Servings: 4
Prep Time: 5 minutes
Cook Time: 10 minutes
Total Ingredients: 7

Nutrition Facts (per serving):
Calories: 250 | Fat: 18g | Carbohy-
drates: 4g | Protein: 18g | Sodium:
430mg | Cholesterol: 85mg

Ingredients:

» 1 lb scallops
» 2 tablespoons vegetable oil
» 3 tablespoons butter
» 3 cloves garlic, minced
» Juice of 1 lemon
» Zest of 1 lemon
» 2 tablespoons fresh parsley, chopped (for garnish)

Preparation:

1. **Prepare the Scallops:** Dry the scallops with paper towels to help them sear properly. Mince the garlic and zest the lemon.

Cooking:

2. **Heat the Wok:** Preheat the wok on medium-high until it starts to give off a bit of smoke.
3. Add the vegetable oil.
4. **Sear the Scallops:** Place the scallops into the wok in a single layer, being cautious not to add too many in. Sear for 2 minutes on each side until they are golden brown and cooked through. Take out of the wok and set aside.
5. **Make the Sauce:** Reduce the heat to medium. Add the butter to the wok and let it melt. Add the minced garlic and cook for 30 seconds until aromatic.
6. **Combine and Finish:** Add the lemon juice and zest to the wok. Bring the scallops back into the wok and gently stir in the sauce to coat them. Cook for 1-2 additional minutes to make sure all ingredients are heated through.

Serving:

7. **Serve the Dish:** Transfer the Lemon Butter Scallops to a plate. Garnish with chopped parsley. Serve with steamed vegetables or rice. Enjoy your elegant and flavorful dish!

TERIYAKI SALMON WITH VEGETABLES

Servings: 4
Prep Time: 10 minutes
Cook Time: 10 minutes
Total Ingredients: 9

Nutrition Facts (per serving):
Calories: 330 | Fat: 14g | Carbohydrates: 16g | Protein: 34g | Sodium: 600mg | Cholesterol: 80mg

Ingredients:

» 4 salmon fillets (about 1 lb total)
» 2 tablespoons vegetable oil
» 1 red bell pepper, sliced
» 1 yellow bell pepper, sliced
» 1 cup snap peas
» 1/2 cup teriyaki sauce
» 2 cloves garlic, minced
» 1 tablespoon grated ginger
» 2 green onions, sliced (for garnish)

Preparation:

1. **Prepare the Ingredients:** Slice the bell peppers and trim the snap peas. Mince the garlic and grate the ginger.

Cooking:

2. **Heat the Wok:** Preheat the wok on medium-high until it starts to give off a bit of smoke. Add 1 tablespoon of vegetable oil.
3. **Cook the Salmon:** Add the salmon fillets to the wok, skin side down if applicable. Cook for 3-4 minutes, then flip and cook for another 3-4 minutes until it is cooked through. Lift the salmon out of the wok and move it onto a plate.
4. **Stir-Fry the Vegetables:** Add the second tablespoon of vegetable oil to the wok. Add the minced garlic and grated ginger, and stir-fry for 30 seconds. Add the bell peppers and snap peas, and stir-fry for 3-4 minutes until they are soft but crisp.
5. **Combine and Add Sauce:** Place the salmon back into the wok. Pour the teriyaki sauce over the salmon and vegetables. Toss gently and cook for another 1-2 minutes.

Serving:

6. **Serve the Dish:** Transfer the Teriyaki Salmon with Vegetables to a platter. Garnish with sliced green onions. Serve immediately with steamed rice. Enjoy your nutritious and flavorful meal!

GINGER-SOY STEAMED FISH

Servings: 4
Prep Time: 10 minutes
Cook Time: 15 minutes
Total Ingredients: 8

Nutrition Facts (per serving):
Calories: 220 | Fat: 7g | Carbohydrates: 4g | Protein: 32g | Sodium: 580mg | Cholesterol: 70mg

Ingredients:

- » 1 lb white fish fillets (such as halibut or snapper)
- » 2 tablespoons soy sauce
- » 1 tablespoon rice vinegar
- » 1 tablespoon sesame oil
- » 2 cloves garlic, minced
- » 1 tablespoon ginger, minced
- » 2 green onions, sliced
- » 1/4 cup fresh cilantro, chopped (for garnish)

Preparation:

1. **Prepare the Fish and Aromatics:** Place the fish fillets on a heatproof plate that fits in your wok. Mince the garlic and ginger. Slice the green onions.

Cooking:

2. **Prepare the Wok:** Add water to the wok and bring it to a boil. Place a steaming rack in the wok, ensuring the water level is below the rack.
3. **Steam the Fish:** In a small bowl, mix the soy sauce, rice vinegar, and sesame oil. Pour the mixture on top of the fish fillets. Sprinkle the minced garlic and ginger over the fish.
4. **Steam:** Place the plate with the fish on the steaming rack. Cover the wok and steam for 10-15 minutes, or until the fish is fully cooked and easily flakes apart with a fork.
5. **Finish:** Gently lift the plate from the wok. Top the fish with the sliced green onions and chopped cilantro.

Serving:

6. **Serve the Dish:** Transfer the Ginger-Soy Steamed Fish to a platter. Serve immediately with steamed rice or a light salad. Enjoy the delicate and aromatic flavors of this healthy dish!

HONEY GLAZED TUNA STEAKS

Servings: 4

Prep Time: 20 minutes (including marinating time of 10 minutes)

Cook Time: 10 minutes

Total Ingredients: 8

Nutrition Facts (per serving):

Calories: 280 | Fat: 12g | Carbohydrates: 10g | Protein: 32g | Sodium: 400mg | Cholesterol: 55mg

Ingredients:

» 4 tuna steaks (about 1 lb total)
» 2 tablespoons vegetable oil
» 3 tablespoons honey
» 2 tablespoons soy sauce
» 1 tablespoon rice vinegar
» 1 tablespoon sesame oil
» 2 cloves garlic, minced
» 1 teaspoon grated fresh ginger

Preparation:

1. **Prepare the Marinade:** In a small bowl, mix together honey, soy sauce, rice vinegar, sesame oil, minced garlic, and grated ginger until well combined.
2. **Marinate the Tuna:** Lay the tuna steaks in a shallow dish and cover them with the marinade. Let them marinate for 10 minutes.

Cooking:

3. **Heat the Wok:** Preheat the wok on medium-high until it begins to smoke slightly. Add the vegetable oil.
4. **Cook the Tuna Steaks:** Place the marinated tuna steaks into the wok. Cook for 2-3 minutes per side until the exterior is seared and the center remains pink. Remove the tuna steaks from the wok and place on a dish.
5. **Thicken the Glaze:** Pour the leftover marinade into the wok. Cook for 2-3 minutes until it thickens into a glaze.

Serving:

6. **Serve the Dish:** Place the tuna steaks on a serving dish and pour the honey glaze over them. Serve with steamed vegetables or a light salad. Enjoy the sweet and savory flavors of your gourmet tuna dish!

Chapter 6
Classic Wok Recipes

Welcome to the Classic Wok Recipes chapter. Here, we take a culinary tour around Asia, discovering timeless dishes that have captivated palates for generations. Each recipe has been carefully chosen to highlight the rich flavors, vibrant colors, and distinct cooking techniques that make wok cuisine so unique. This chapter is designed to help you build on the skills you've developed and explore some of the most beloved classic recipes in a beginner-friendly way.

Chinese Cuisine

Chinese wok cooking is renowned for its bold flavors and diverse ingredients. These recipes bring the essence of Chinese street food and family dinners to your kitchen.

SPICY KUNG PAO CHICKEN DELIGHT

Spicy Kung Pao Chicken Delight is a hot, savory dish made with tender chicken pieces, crunchy peanuts, colorful vegetables, and a bold, flavorful sauce. This classic recipe strikes a balance between spice and sweetness, offering a flavor explosion with each bite. It is a Sichuan culinary classic, known for its vibrant flavors and satisfying texture.

Servings: 4

Prep Time: 45 minutes (including marinating time of 30 minutes)

Cook Time: 15 minutes

Total Ingredients: 11

Nutrition Facts (per serving):

Calories: 290 | Fat: 12g | Carbohydrates: 15g | Protein: 26g | Sodium: 650mg | Cholesterol: 70mg

Ingredients:

» 1 lb skinless, boneless chicken thighs, diced into small pieces
» 2 tablespoons soy sauce
» 1 tablespoon rice vinegar
» 1 tablespoon cornstarch
» 2 tablespoons vegetable oil, divided
» 1/2 cup unsalted peanuts
» 4 dried red chilies, cut in half
» 1 red bell pepper, diced
» 3 cloves garlic, minced
» 1 tablespoon ginger, minced
» 2 tablespoons hoisin sauce
» 1 teaspoon sugar

Preparation:

1. **Marinate the Chicken:** Put the chicken pieces in a bowl and mix with the cornstarch, rice vinegar, and soy sauce. After thoroughly mixing, place it in the fridge to marinate for at least half an hour.

Cooking:

2. **Prepare the Ingredients:** As the chicken marinates, prepare the rest of your ingredients. Dice the bell pepper, mince the garlic and ginger, and cut the dried red chilies.

3. **Cook the Chicken:** In the wok, heat up 1 tablespoon of vegetable oil on high heat. Add the marinated chicken and stir-fry for 5 to 7 minutes, until the chicken is cooked through and golden brown. Take the chicken out of the wok and set it aside.

4. **Stir-Fry the Aromatics and Peppers:**
   - Fill the wok with the remaining tablespoon of vegetable oil. Add and stir-fry the dried red chilies for approximately 30 seconds until fragrant. Pay attention not to burn them.
   - Add the minced garlic and ginger, and stir-fry for 30 more seconds.
   - Toss in the diced red bell pepper, and stir-fry for 2-3 minutes until they are cooked through but still crunchy.

5. **Combine and Finish the Dish:**
   - Place the cooked chicken back in the wok. Add the peanuts and stir everything together.
   - Combine hoisin sauce and sugar In a small bowl. Pour this sauce into the wok and stir well to coat all the ingredients.
   » Cook for a further 2-3 minutes until everything is well cooked and combined.

Serving:

6. **Serve the Dish:** Transfer the Kung Pao Chicken to a serving platter. Serve immediately with steamed rice or your favorite side dish. Enjoy your flavorful, spicy creation!

SAVORY BEEF AND BROCCOLI STIR-FRY

Savory Beef and Broccoli Stir-Fry is one of the most popular dishes in the Chinese-American cuisine. It combines tender beef with crunchy broccoli in a rich, umami-packed sauce. The pleasant contrast created by the mix of crisp broccoli and tender meat makes it perfect for a weeknight dinner.

Servings: 4

Prep Time: 35 minutes (including marinating time of 20 minutes)

Cook Time: 15 minutes

Total Number of Ingredients: 11

Nutrition Facts (per serving):
Calories: 310 | Fat: 14g | Carbohydrates: 18g | Protein: 27g | Sodium: 750mg | Cholesterol: 60mg

Ingredients

- » 1 lb flank steak, thinly sliced against the grain
- » 2 tablespoons soy sauce
- » 1 tablespoon oyster sauce
- » 1 tablespoon cornstarch
- » 2 tablespoons vegetable oil, divided
- » 1 large head of broccoli, cut into florets
- » 3 cloves garlic, minced
- » 1 tablespoon ginger, minced
- » 1/4 cup beef broth
- » 2 tablespoons hoisin sauce
- » 1 teaspoon sugar

Preparation

1. **Marinate the Beef:** In a mixing bowl, combine the sliced beef with soy sauce, oyster sauce, and cornstarch. Mix well and let it sit in the fridge for at least 20 minutes to marinate.

Cooking

2. **Prepare the Ingredients:** While the beef is marinating, prepare the rest of your ingredients. Cut the broccoli into florets, mince the garlic and ginger.
3. **Blanch the Broccoli:** In a saucepan, bring the water to a boil. Add the broccoli florets and blanch for 2 minutes until bright green and slightly tender. Drain and place aside.
4. **Cook the Beef:** In the wok, heat up 1 tablespoon of vegetable oil on high heat. After adding the marinated beef, stir-fry it for 4–5 minutes, until it is browned and cooked through. Take the beef out of the wok and set it aside.
5. **Stir-Fry the Aromatics:** Add the remaining tablespoon of vegetable oil to the wok. Stir-fry the ginger and minced garlic for about 30 seconds until fragrant.
6. **Combine and Finish the Dish:**
   - Add the blanched broccoli to the wok and stir to combine with the aromatics.
   - Return the cooked beef to the wok. In a small bowl, combine beef broth, hoisin sauce, and sugar. Pour this sauce into the wok and stir well to coat all the ingredients.
   - Cook for an additional 2-3 minutes until all ingredients are heated throughout and well combined.

Serving

7. **Serve the Dish:** Transfer the Beef and Broccoli Stir-Fry to a serving platter. Serve immediately with noodles or steamed rice. Enjoy your delicious, savory creation!

TANGY PINEAPPLE PORK

Tangy Pineapple Pork is all about the balance of opposing tastes. The crispy pork pieces, coated in a tangy pineapple sauce, are paired with bell peppers and pineapples, creating a delightful and colorful meal. This dish perfectly captures the harmony between sweet and savory that is central to Chinese cooking.

Servings: 4

Prep Time: 35 minutes (including marinating time of 15 minutes)

Cook Time: 20 minutes

Total Number of Ingredients: 13

Nutrition Facts (per serving):
Calories: 450 | Fat: 20g | Carbohydrates: 45g | Protein: 25g | Sodium: 800mg | Cholesterol: 70mg

Ingredients:

- » 1 lb pork tenderloin, sliced into small pieces
- » 1 tablespoon soy sauce
- » 1 tablespoon rice wine or dry sherry
- » 1 egg white
- » 1/2 cup cornstarch
- » 1/4 cup vegetable oil, for frying
- » 1 red bell pepper, cut into pieces
- » 1 green bell pepper, cut into pieces
- » 1 cup of fresh or canned pineapple pieces
- » 3 cloves garlic, minced
- » 1/4 cup ketchup
- » 1/4 cup rice vinegar
- » 1/4 cup sugar
- » 2 tablespoons soy sauce
- » 1 tablespoon cornstarch and 2 tablespoons of water combined (slurry)

Preparation:

1. **Marinate the Pork:** In a bowl, mix the pork pieces with soy sauce, rice wine or dry sherry, and egg white. Leave it in the fridge to marinate for a minimum of 15 minutes.

Cooking:

2. **Prepare the Ingredients:** While the pork is marinating, cut the bell peppers into chunks, prepare the pineapple chunks, and mince the garlic.
3. **Coat the Pork:** After marinating, coat the pork pieces with cornstarch, shaking off any excess.
4. **Fry the Pork:** Heat the vegetable oil in the wok over medium-high flame. Fry the pork pieces in batches until golden and crispy, about 3-4 minutes per batch. Remove and use paper towels to drain.
5. **Stir-Fry the Vegetables:** Take out all except 1 tablespoon of the wok's oil. Stir-fry the minced garlic for 30 seconds until fragrant. Add the red and green bell peppers and stir-fry for 2-3 minutes until they start to soften.
6. **Prepare the Sauce:** In a small bowl, mix ketchup, rice vinegar, sugar, and soy sauce.
7. **Combine and Finish the Dish:**
   - Return the crispy pork to the wok along with the pineapple chunks.
   - Pour the sauce over the pork and vegetables, stirring to ensure that everything is uniformly coated.
   - Add the cornstarch slurry to the wok and cook for 1-2 more minutes until the sauce thickens and becomes glossy.

Serving:

8. **Serve the Dish:** Transfer the Tangy Pineapple Pork to a serving platter. Serve immediately with noodles or steamed rice. Enjoy the perfect balance of tangy, sweet, and savory flavors!

Japanese Cuisine

Japanese wok cooking emphasizes harmony and simplicity, bringing out the natural flavors of fresh ingredients. These dishes offer a taste of traditional Japanese comfort food, ideal for making nutritious and yummy meals at home.

YAKISOBA NOODLES: FLAVORFUL STIR-FRIED NOODLE DELIGHT

Yakisoba is a popular Japanese stir-fried noodle dish, combining savory noodles with a variety of vegetables and a tangy, savory sauce. It's a versatile dish perfect for a quick weeknight meal.

Servings: 4

Prep Time: 15 minutes

Cook Time: 15 minutes

Total Number of Ingredients: 11

Nutrition Facts (per serving):

Calories: 400 | Fat: 12g | Carbohydrates: 58g | Protein: 12g | Sodium: 900mg | Cholesterol: 0mg

Ingredients:

- » 8 oz yakisoba noodles (fresh or pre-cooked)
- » 2 tbsp vegetable oil
- » 1/2 lb chicken breast, cut very thinly
- » 1 small onion, cut very thinly
- » 1 medium carrot, cut into thin strips
- » 1/2 green bell pepper, cut very thinly
- » 1/2 red bell pepper, cut very thinly
- » 1/4 cup yakisoba sauce (store-bought or homemade)
- » 2 tbsp soy sauce
- » 2 green onions, chopped
- » 1 tbsp sesame seeds (optional)
- » 1 tbsp sesame seeds (optional)

Preparation:

1. **Prepare the Ingredients:** Slice the chicken breast into thin strips. Thinly slice the onion and bell peppers, cut the carrot into thin strips and chop the green onions.

Cooking:

2. **Cook the Chicken:** In a wok heat 1 tbsp of vegetable oil over medium-high heat. Add the chicken strips and stir-fry until fully cooked, for 5-7 minutes. Take out of the wok and put aside.
3. **Cook the Vegetables:** Add the remaining tablespoon of vegetable oil to the wok. Add the onion, carrot, and bell peppers. Stir-fry for 3-4 minutes until the vegetables are tender-crisp.
4. **Combine Noodles and Sauce:**
5. Add the yakisoba noodles to the wok, tossing them with the vegetables.
6. Pour in the yakisoba sauce and soy sauce. Stir well to coat the noodles and vegetables evenly.
7. Add the cooked chicken back to the wok and combine everything together. Add 2-3 more minutes of cooking time until everything is hot.

Serving:

8. **Garnish and Serve:** Transfer the yakisoba to serving plates. Sprinkle chopped green onions and sesame seeds on top, if using. Serve immediately and enjoy your flavorful stir-fried noodle delight!

TERIYAKI CHICKEN STIR-FRY: SWEET AND SAVORY PERFECTION

This Teriyaki Chicken Stir-Fry balances the sweet and savory flavors of its rich teriyaki sauce, combined with tender chicken and crisp vegetables for a delightful meal.

Servings: 4

Prep Time: 25 minutes (including marinating time of 10 minutes)

Cook Time: 15 minutes

Ingredients: 10

Nutrition Facts (per serving):
Calories: 320 | Fat: 12g | Carbohydrates: 20g | Protein: 30g | Sodium: 720mg | Cholesterol: 70mg

Ingredients:

- » 1 lb boneless, skinless chicken thighs, cut into small pieces
- » 1/4 cup soy sauce
- » 1/4 cup mirin
- » 2 tablespoons sugar
- » 1 tablespoon sake (optional)
- » 2 tablespoons vegetable oil
- » 1 small onion, sliced
- » 1 bell pepper, sliced
- » 2 cups broccoli florets
- » 1 tablespoon cornstarch and 2 tablespoons of water combined (slurry)
- » Sesame seeds and sliced green onions for garnish

Preparation:

1. **Marinate the Chicken:** In a bowl, mix the soy sauce, mirin, sugar, and sake (if using). Add the chicken pieces and marinate for 10 minutes.
2. **Prepare the Vegetables:** Slice the onion and bell pepper. Cut the broccoli into florets.

Cooking:

3. **Heat the Wok:** Set the wok on medium-high and pour 1 tablespoon of vegetable oil. Cook until the oil starts to smoke slightly.
4. **Cook the Chicken:** Add the marinated chicken to the wok and stir-fry until fully cooked and slightly caramelized, for 5-7 minutes. Take the chicken out and set it aside.
5. **Stir-Fry the Vegetables:** Add the remaining tablespoon of oil to the wok. Stir-fry the onion and bell pepper for about 2 minutes. Add the broccoli florets and continue to stir-fry for another 3-4 minutes until the vegetables are tender-crisp.
6. **Combine and Thicken:** Add the cooked chicken back to the wok. Pour in any remaining marinade. Add the cornstarch slurry and stir well to thicken the sauce, cooking for another 2 minutes.

Serving:

7. **Garnish and Serve:** Sprinkle sliced green onions and sesame seeds on top. Serve hot with steamed rice or noodles.

TEMPURA VEGETABLE MEDLEY: LIGHT AND CRISPY VEGGIE TREATS

Tempura Vegetable Medley offers a delightful assortment of vegetables coated in a light, crispy batter, perfect for an appetizer or a side dish.

Servings: 4
Prep Time: 20 minutes
Cook Time: 15 minutes
Ingredients: 12

Nutrition Facts (per serving):
Calories: 250 | Fat: 14g | Carbohydrates: 28g | Protein: 4g | Sodium: 300mg | Cholesterol: 0mg

Ingredients:

- » 1 small sweet potato, peeled and thinly sliced
- » 1 small zucchini, sliced into thin rounds
- » 1 red bell pepper, sliced into strips
- » 1 small broccoli head, cut into florets
- » 1 small onion, sliced into rings
- » 1 cup all-purpose flour
- » 1 egg, lightly beaten
- » 1 cup ice-cold water
- » 1/2 cup cornstarch
- » Vegetable oil for frying
- » Salt for seasoning
- » Soy sauce or tempura dipping sauce for serving

Preparation:

1. **Prepare the Vegetables:** Slice the sweet potato, zucchini, and red bell pepper. Cut the broccoli into florets and slice the onion into rings. Pat the vegetables dry with paper towels to get rid of excess water.
2. **Make the Batter:** In a bowl, lightly beat the egg and mix it with ice-cold water. Add the all-purpose flour and cornstarch, mixing gently until just combined. The batter should be a little lumpy.

Cooking:

3. **Heat the Oil:** In a deep wok, heat vegetable oil to 350°F. Use a thermometer to maintain the temperature.
4. **Fry the Vegetables:**
5. Dip the prepared vegetables into the batter, shaking off any excess.
6. Fry in small batches to avoid overcrowding, cooking each batch for 2-3 minutes until light and crispy.
7. Use a slotted spoon or spider skimmer to take the tempura out of the oil, draining on paper towels to remove excess oil.

Serving:

8. **Season and Serve:** Lightly season the tempura with salt while still hot. Serve immediately with soy sauce or tempura dipping sauce.

Thai Cuisine

Thai wok cooking is celebrated for its harmonious balance of sweet, sour, salty, and spicy flavors. These recipes transport the colorful and fragrant spirit of Thai street food and home-cooked meals to your kitchen.

RED CURRY CHICKEN: CREAMY AND SPICY THAI CLASSIC

Red Curry Chicken is a quintessential Thai dish recognized for its rich, creamy coconut base and vibrant, fiery red curry paste. This dish perfectly balances the heat of red chilies with the softness of coconut milk, resulting in a mouthwatering experience that is both robust and comforting.

Servings: 4
Prep Time: 10 minutes
Cook Time: 15 minutes
Total Ingredients: 8

Nutrition Facts (per serving):
Calories: 350 | Fat: 20g | Carbohydrates: 10g | Protein: 28g | Sodium: 600mg | Cholesterol: 75mg

Ingredients:

» 1 lb boneless, skinless chicken thighs, cut into small pieces
» 2 tablespoons red curry paste
» 1 can (14 oz) coconut milk
» 1 red bell pepper, sliced
» 1 cup green beans, trimmed
» 2 tablespoons fish sauce
» 1 tablespoon brown sugar
» Fresh basil leaves, for garnish

Preparation:

1. **Prep the Ingredients:** Cut the chicken thighs into small pieces. Slice the red bell pepper and trim the green beans.

Cooking:

2. **Heat the Wok:** Preheat the wok on medium-high until it begins to smoke slightly.
3. **Cook the Chicken:** Add the red curry paste to the wok and stir-fry for 1-2 minutes until fragrant. Add the chicken pieces and stir-fry until they are lightly browned, about 3-4 minutes.
4. **Add the Coconut Milk:** Pour in the coconut milk and mix well to combine.
5. **Add the Vegetables:** Add the sliced red bell pepper and green beans.
6. **Season and Simmer:** Add the fish sauce and brown sugar and stir. After bringing to a simmer, cook for a further 5-7 minutes until the chicken is thoroughly cooked and the vegetables are soft.

Serving:

7. **Garnish and Serve:**
   • Take off the heat and garnish with fresh basil leaves. Serve with steamed jasmine rice or your preferred side. Enjoy your creamy and spicy Red Curry Chicken!

CLASSIC PAD THAI: SWEET AND TANGY NOODLE SENSATION

Pad Thai is a quintessential Thai stir-fried noodle dish known for its harmonious blend of sweet, tangy, and savory flavors. This popular street food is perfect for a quick and satisfying meal.

Servings: 4
Prep Time: 20 minutes
Cook Time: 15 minutes
Total Ingredients: 13

Nutrition Facts (per serving):
Calories: 450 | Fat: 18g | Carbohydrates: 50g | Protein: 20g | Sodium: 900mg | Cholesterol: 150mg

Ingredients:

- » 8 oz rice noodles
- » 2 tbsp vegetable oil
- » 1 lb chicken breast, thinly sliced
- » 2 eggs, lightly beaten
- » 1 cup bean sprouts
- » 1/2 cup carrots, julienned
- » 1/2 cup green onions, chopped
- » 1/4 cup crushed peanuts
- » 1/4 cup fresh cilantro, chopped
- » 2 tbsp tamarind paste
- » 2 tbsp fish sauce
- » 1 tbsp soy sauce
- » 1 tbsp sugar
- » Lime wedges, for serving

Preparation

1. **Prepare the Noodles:** Give the rice noodles a good 20 minutes to soften in warm water. Pour off and set aside.
2. **Prepare the Sauce:** In a small bowl, mix fish sauce, soy sauce, tamarind paste and sugar until well combined. Leave aside.

Cooking

3. **Cook the Chicken:** Heat 1 tablespoon of vegetable oil in a wok over medium-high heat. Add the chicken slices and stir-fry until cooked through, about 5-7 minutes. Remove from the wok and set aside.
4. **Cook the Eggs:** Add another tablespoon of oil to the wok. Spoon in the beaten eggs and scramble until just set. Push the eggs to the side of the wok.
5. **Stir-Fry the Noodles:** Add the soaked noodles to the wok, pouring the sauce over the noodles. Stir thoroughly to coat the noodles with the sauce.
6. **Combine Ingredients:** Add the cooked chicken back into the wok along with the bean sprouts, green onions, and carrots. Stir-fry for another 3-5 minutes until everything is well combined and heated through.

Serving

7. **Garnish and Serve:** Transfer the Pad Thai to serving plates. Sprinkle with crushed peanuts and fresh cilantro. Serve with lime wedges on the side for an extra tangy kick.

THAI BASIL BEEF STIR-FRY: FRESH AND FLAVORFUL

This Thai Basil Beef Stir-Fry brings together tender slices of beef, aromatic basil, and vibrant vegetables in a deliciously savory sauce. It's a quick and satisfying dish that's perfect for busy weeknights.

Servings: 4

Prep Time: 25 minutes (including marinating time of 10 minutes)

Cook Time: 15 minutes

Total Ingredients: 10

Nutrition Facts (per serving):
Calories: 360 | Fat: 18g | Carbohydrates: 20g | Protein: 30g | Sodium: 800mg | Cholesterol: 70mg

Ingredients:

- » 1 lb beef sirloin, thinly sliced
- » 2 tbsp vegetable oil
- » 3 cloves garlic, minced
- » 1 red bell pepper, sliced
- » 1 green bell pepper, sliced
- » 1 onion, thinly sliced
- » 1 cup fresh Thai basil leaves
- » 2 tbsp soy sauce
- » 2 tbsp oyster sauce
- » 1 tbsp fish sauce
- » 1 tbsp brown sugar

Preparation:

1. **Prep the Ingredients:**
   - Thinly slice the beef sirloin. Mince the garlic, slice the red and green bell peppers, and thinly slice the onion. Wash and dry the Thai basil leaves.
2. **Marinate the Beef:**
   - In a bowl, combine the sliced beef with 1 tablespoon of soy sauce and let it marinate for about 10 minutes.

Cooking:

3. **Stir-Fry the Beef:**
   - Heat 1 tablespoon of vegetable oil in a wok over medium-high heat. Add and stir-fry the marinated beef until it's browned and just cooked through, around 2-3 minutes. Take the beef out of the wok and set it aside.
4. **Cook the Vegetables:**
   - Pour the remaining tablespoon of vegetable oil into the wok. Add the minced garlic and stir-fry until fragrant, for 30 seconds. Add the sliced bell peppers and onion, and stir-fry until they start to soften, about 3-4 minutes.
5. **Combine and Season:**
   - Add the beef back to the wok. Add the oyster sauce, fish sauce, remaining soy sauce, and brown sugar. Stir thoroughly to combine all of the ingredients.
6. **Add Thai Basil:**
   - Add the Thai basil leaves and stir until they are wilted and the dish is heated through.

Serving:

7. **Serve:** Serve the Thai Basil Beef Stir-Fry hot over steamed jasmine rice. Garnish with extra Thai basil leaves if desired.

Korean Cuisine

Korean cuisine is renowned for its vibrant and dynamic flavors, which combine spicy, savory, sweet, and tangy elements to create dishes that are both exciting and comforting. These recipes introduce you to some classic Korean dishes that are ideal for a delicious meal at home and are suitable for beginners.

SAVORY BEEF BULGOGI STIR-FRY

Experience the perfect blend of sweet and tangy flavors with this beginner-friendly Beef Bulgogi Stir-Fry. A staple in Korean cuisine, this dish combines tender beef with aromatic vegetables and a savory marinade, creating a delightful meal that's both satisfying and easy to prepare.

Servings: 4

Prep Time: 50 minutes (including marinating time of 30 minutes)

Cook Time: 10 minutes

Total Number of Ingredients: 11

Nutrition Facts (per serving):
Calories: 320 | Fat: 12g | Carbohydrates: 20g | Protein: 30g | Sodium: 700mg | Cholesterol: 60mg

Ingredients

» 1 lb beef sirloin, thinly sliced
» 1/4 cup soy sauce
» 2 tablespoons brown sugar
» 1 tablespoon sesame oil
» 1 tablespoon vegetable oil
» 4 cloves garlic, minced
» 1 medium onion, thinly sliced
» 1 medium carrot, julienned
» 1 bell pepper, thinly cut
» 2 green onions, chopped
» 1 tablespoon sesame seeds, toasted

Preparation:

1. **Marinate the Beef:** In a large bowl, combine soy sauce, brown sugar, sesame oil, and minced garlic. Add the thinly sliced beef and mix well to coat evenly. Cover and marinate in the fridge for 30 minutes, or up to 2 hours to add more taste.
2. **Prepare the Vegetables:** While the beef is in the marinade, slice the onion, julienne the carrot, and thinly slice the bell pepper. Chop the green onions.

Cooking:

3. **Stir-Fry the Beef:** In a wok heat vegetable oil over high heat until it shimmers. Add the marinated beef and stir-fry for about 3-4 minutes until the beef is browned and cooked through. Take out and put aside the beef from the wok.
4. **Cook the Vegetables:** In the same wok, add the onion, carrot, and bell pepper. Stir-fry for about 2-3 minutes until the vegetables are tender-crisp.
5. **Combine Ingredients:** Add the cooked beef back into the wok and mix well with the vegetables. Add 1-2 minutes of stir-frying until everything is hot.

Serving:

6. **Garnish and Serve:** Transfer the beef bulgogi stir-fry to a serving plate. Sprinkle with chopped green onions and toasted sesame seeds. Serve hot, ideally with steamed rice or as a filling for lettuce wraps.

BIBIMBAP: KOREAN MIXED RICE BOWL

Bibimbap is a versatile and colorful Korean dish featuring a mix of rice, sautéed vegetables, and a fried egg, all brought together with a flavorful gochujang sauce.

Servings: 4

Prep Time: 20 minutes

Cook Time: 20 minutes

Total Number of Ingredients: 10

Nutrition Facts (per serving):
Calories: 450 | Fat: 12g | Carbohydrates: 65g | Protein: 15g | Sodium: 800mg | Cholesterol: 30mg

Ingredients

»   2 cups cooked white rice
»   1 cup spinach, blanched
»   1 carrot, julienned
»   1 zucchini, julienned
»   1 cup mushrooms, sliced
»   1 cup bean sprouts, blanched
»   4 eggs
»   2 tablespoons soy sauce
»   2 tablespoons sesame oil
»   2 tablespoons gochujang (Korean red chili paste)

Preparation:

1. **Prepare the Vegetables:** Julienne the carrot and zucchini. Slice the mushrooms. Blanch the bean sprouts and spinach in boiling water for 1 minute each, then remove the water and set aside.

Cooking:

2. **Cook the Vegetables:** In a wok, heat 1 tablespoon of sesame oil on medium-high. Stir-fry the carrots, zucchini, and mushrooms separately for about 3-4 minutes each until tender. Season each with a little soy sauce.

3. **Cook the Eggs:** In the same wok, fry the eggs sunny-side up. Set aside.

Serving:

4. **Assemble the Bibimbap:** Prepare four bowls with the cooked rice. Arrange the vegetables (spinach, carrot, zucchini, mushrooms, bean sprouts) on top of the rice. Place a fried egg on top of each bowl.

5. **Add Sauce:** Add a dollop of gochujang and drizzle with the remaining sesame oil.

6. **Mix and Enjoy:** Mix everything together before eating and enjoy the colorful, flavorful harmony of Bibimbap!

SPICY KIMCHI TOFU STIR-FRY: A FLAVORFUL TOFU DISH

Spicy Kimchi Tofu Stir-Fry combines the heat and tang of kimchi with the soft texture of tofu, creating a dish that's both satisfying and full of flavor. This recipe is perfect for those looking to add a spicy, plant-based option to their meal repertoire.

Servings: 4
Prep Time: 10 minutes
Cook Time: 15 minutes
Total Ingredients: 8

Nutrition Facts (per serving):
Calories: 250 | Fat: 12g | Carbohydrates: 18g | Protein: 15g | Sodium: 750mg | Cholesterol: 0mg

Ingredients:

- » 1 block (14 oz) firm tofu, drained and cut into cubes
- » 1 cup kimchi, chopped
- » 1 tablespoon kimchi juice
- » 2 tablespoons vegetable oil
- » 1 tablespoon gochujang (Korean red chili paste)
- » 2 green onions, sliced
- » 1 tablespoon soy sauce
- » 1 teaspoon sesame oil

Preparation:

1. **Prep the Ingredients:** Drain and cube the tofu. Chop the kimchi and slice the green onions.

Cooking:

2. **Heat the Wok:** Set the wok on medium-high heat and heat it up until it starts to smoke slightly.
3. **Cook the Tofu:** Put in 1 tablespoon of vegetable oil. Add the tofu cubes. It will take about 5 to 7 minutes of stir-frying until they are golden brown on all sides. Take the tofu out of the wok and set it aside.
4. **Cook the Kimchi:** Add the remaining 1 tablespoon of vegetable oil to the wok. Add the chopped kimchi and stir-fry for 2-3 minutes until it becomes fragrant and slightly caramelized.
5. **Combine and Season:** Place the tofu back in the wok. Add the kimchi juice, gochujang, and soy sauce. Stir well to evenly coat the tofu and kimchi with the sauce. Stir-fry for another 2-3 minutes until all ingredients are well combined and fully heated.
6. **Finish the Dish:** Drizzle sesame oil over the stir-fry and toss to combine.

Serving:

7. **Serve the Dish:** Transfer the Spicy Kimchi Tofu Stir-Fry onto a dish for serving. Garnish with sliced green onions. Serve with steamed rice or a side of vegetables. Enjoy your flavorful and spicy tofu dish!

Chapter 7
Complementary Dishes and Treats

This chapter will help you round out your meals with a variety of salads, sauces, snacks, and desserts that pair perfectly with your wok-cooked dishes. Whether you're looking for a refreshing side salad, a flavorful sauce to enhance your main course, a light snack, or a sweet ending to your meal, you'll find it here.

SPICY SZECHUAN SAUCE

Servings: 4

Prep Time: 5 minutes

Cook Time: 10 minutes

Total Ingredients: 9

Nutrition Facts (per serving): Calories: 70 | Fat: 2g | Carbohydrates: 12g | Protein: 2g | Sodium: 600mg | Sugar: 8g

Ingredients:

»   2 tablespoons soy sauce
»   2 tablespoons rice vinegar
»   2 tablespoons hoisin sauce
»   1 tablespoon chili paste (such as sambal oelek)
»   1 tablespoon sugar
»   1 teaspoon Szechuan peppercorns, toasted and ground
»   2 cloves garlic, minced
»   1 teaspoon ginger, minced
»   2 tablespoons of water and 1 teaspoon of cornstarch (optional for thickening)

Preparation:

1. **Mix the Base:** In a small bowl, mix together the soy sauce, rice vinegar, hoisin sauce, chili paste, and sugar. Stir until the sugar is dissolved.
2. **Prepare Aromatics:** Mince the garlic and ginger, and toast and grind the Szechuan peppercorns.

Cooking:

3. **Heat Aromatics:** Heat a small saucepan over medium heat. Add the garlic, ginger, and ground Szechuan peppercorns. Stir-fry for about 1-2 minutes until fragrant.
4. **Combine and Thicken:** Add the soy sauce mixture and heat until it begins to boil. If you prefer a thicker sauce, add the cornstarch slurry and cook for 1-2 minutes until it thickens.

Serving:

5. **Use the Sauce:** Use this Spicy Szechuan Sauce immediately in your favorite stir-fry dishes or as a dipping sauce for dumplings and spring rolls. Enjoy the bold flavors and fiery heat!

HOISIN-PEANUT SAUCE

Servings: 4
Prep Time: 5 minutes
Cook Time: 5 minutes
Total Ingredients: 7

Nutrition Facts (per serving): Calories: 90 | Fat: 6g | Carbohydrates: 8g | Protein: 3g | Sodium: 400mg | Sugar: 3g

Ingredients:

» 3 tablespoons hoisin sauce
» 2 tablespoons smooth peanut butter
» 1 tablespoon soy sauce
» 1 tablespoon rice vinegar
» 1 tablespoon honey
» 2 cloves garlic, minced
» 2-3 tablespoons water (to adjust consistency)

Preparation:
1. **Combine Ingredients:** In a small bowl, combine hoisin sauce, peanut butter, soy sauce, rice vinegar, honey, and minced garlic.

Cooking:
2. **Blend and Adjust:** Whisk the ingredients until smooth and well combined. Gradually add water, one tablespoon at a time, until the desired consistency is achieved.

Serving:
3. **Serve the Sauce:** Use this Hoisin-Peanut Sauce as a dip for spring rolls, a dressing for salads, or a sauce for noodles and stir-fries. Enjoy the rich, nutty flavor it brings to your meals!

SWEET CHILI SAUCE

Servings: 4
Prep Time: 5 minutes
Cook Time: 10 minutes
Total Ingredients: 7

Nutrition Facts (per serving): Calories: 50 | Fat: 0g | Carbohydrates: 12g | Protein: 0g | Sodium: 250mg | Sugar: 10g

Ingredients:

» 1/2 cup rice vinegar
» 1/2 cup sugar
» 1/4 cup water
» 2 tablespoons fish sauce
» 1 tablespoon chili paste (such as sambal oelek)
» 2 cloves garlic, minced
» 1 teaspoon cornstarch mixed with 1 tablespoon water (optional, for thickening)

Preparation:
1. **Mix Ingredients:** In a small saucepan, mix together sugar, rice vinegar, water, fish sauce, and chili paste. Stir until sugar is dissolved.

Cooking:
2. **Simmer Sauce:** Heat the mixture until it boils, over medium heat. Once boiling, add the minced garlic and lower the heat to maintain a simmer. Cook for 5-7 minutes until slightly thickened.
3. **Thicken Sauce (optional):** If a thicker sauce is desired, stir in the cornstarch slurry and cook for 1-2 minutes until the desired consistency is achieved.

Serving:
4. **Serve the Sauce:** Use this Sweet Chili Sauce as a dipping sauce for spring rolls, a glaze for grilled meats, or a drizzle over stir-fried vegetables. Enjoy the perfect balance of sweet and spicy!

SESAME-GINGER DRESSING

Servings: 4
Prep Time: 5 minutes
Total Ingredients: 7

Nutrition Facts (per serving): Calories: 60 | Fat: 5g | Carbohydrates: 4g | Protein: 1g | Sodium: 300mg | Sugar: 2g

Ingredients:

- » 2 tablespoons soy sauce
- » 2 tablespoons rice vinegar
- » 1 tablespoon sesame oil
- » 1 tablespoon honey
- » 1 teaspoon grated fresh ginger
- » 1 teaspoon sesame seeds
- » 1 clove garlic, minced

Preparation:

1. **Combine Ingredients:** Combine soy sauce, rice vinegar, sesame oil, honey, grated ginger, sesame seeds and chopped garlic in a small bowl and whisk until well blended.

Serving:

2. **Use the Dressing:** Drizzle this Sesame-Ginger Dressing over salads, use it as a marinade for meats, or serve it as a dipping sauce for vegetables and spring rolls. Enjoy the fresh and nutty flavors it brings to your dishes!

CITRUS PONZU SAUCE

Servings: 4
Prep Time: 5 minutes
Total Ingredients: 6

Nutrition Facts (per serving): Calories: 30 | Fat: 0g | Carbohydrates: 6g | Protein: 1g | Sodium: 400mg | Sugar: 3g

Ingredients:

- » 3 tablespoons soy sauce
- » 2 tablespoons lemon juice
- » 2 tablespoons lime juice
- » 1 tablespoon rice vinegar
- » 1 tablespoon mirin
- » 1 teaspoon grated fresh ginger

Preparation:

1. **Mix Ingredients:** In a bowl, mix together soy sauce, lemon juice, lime juice, rice vinegar, mirin, and grated ginger. Whisk until well blended.

Serving:

2. **Use the Sauce:** Use this Citrus Ponzu Sauce as a dipping sauce for dumplings, a marinade for meats and fish, or a drizzle over salads and stir-fries. Enjoy the bright and tangy flavors!

ASIAN CUCUMBER SALAD

Servings: 4
Prep Time: 10 minutes
Total Ingredients: 7

Nutrition Facts (per serving): Calories: 40 | Fat: 2g | Carbohydrates: 5g | Protein: 1g | Sodium: 200mg | Sugar: 2g

Ingredients:

» 2 large cucumbers, thinly sliced
» 2 tablespoons rice vinegar
» 1 tablespoon soy sauce
» 1 tablespoon sesame oil
» 1 teaspoon sugar
» 1 teaspoon sesame seeds
» 1 green onion, sliced

Preparation:

1. **Prepare the Cucumbers:** Slice the cucumbers thinly and transfer them to a large bowl.
2. **Make the Dressing:** In a small bowl, combine rice vinegar, soy sauce, sesame oil, and sugar, whisking until the sugar fully dissolves.
3. **Combine:** Drizzle the dressing over the cucumbers. Add the sesame seeds and sliced green onion. Toss everything together until the cucumbers are well coated with the dressing.
4. **Chill:** Refrigerate the salad for at least 10 minutes to allow the flavors to blend.

Serving:

5. **Serve:** Serve the Asian Cucumber Salad chilled, garnished with additional sesame seeds if desired. Enjoy this crisp and refreshing salad as a side dish or light snack.

SPICY THAI PAPAYA SALAD

Servings: 4
Prep Time: 15 minutes
Total Ingredients: 9

Nutrition Facts (per serving): Calories: 70 | Fat: 3g | Carbohydrates: 10g | Protein: 2g | Sodium: 300mg | Sugar: 6g

Ingredients:

» 1 green papaya, peeled and shredded
» 1 carrot, shredded
» 1 cup cherry tomatoes, halved
» 1/4 cup roasted peanuts
» 2 tablespoons lime juice
» 2 tablespoons fish sauce
» 1 tablespoon palm sugar (or brown sugar)
» 2 garlic cloves, minced
» 1-2 Thai chilies, minced

Preparation:

1. **Prepare the Vegetables:** Peel and shred the green papaya and carrot. Place them in a large bowl. Add the halved cherry tomatoes and roasted peanuts.
2. **Make the Dressing:** In a small bowl, whisk together lime juice, fish sauce, palm sugar, minced garlic, and minced Thai chilies until well combined.
3. **Combine:** Drizzle the dressing over the shredded papaya and carrots. Mix everything together thoroughly until the dressing evenly coats all the ingredients.

Serving:

4. **Serve:** Serve the Spicy Thai Papaya Salad immediately, garnished with additional roasted peanuts if desired. Enjoy this tangy and spicy salad as a refreshing side dish.

SESAME GINGER SLAW

Servings: 4
Prep Time: 10 minutes
Total Ingredients: 8

Nutrition Facts (per serving): Calories: 60 | Fat: 4g | Carbohydrates: 7g | Protein: 1g | Sodium: 220mg | Sugar: 3g

Ingredients:

- » 2 cups shredded cabbage (green or purple)
- » 1 cup shredded carrots
- » 1/4 cup sliced red bell pepper
- » 1/4 cup sliced green onions
- » 2 tablespoons rice vinegar
- » 1 tablespoon soy sauce
- » 1 tablespoon sesame oil
- » 1 teaspoon grated fresh ginger

Preparation:

1. **Prepare the Vegetables:** In a large bowl, combine shredded cabbage, shredded carrots, sliced red bell pepper, and sliced green onions.
2. **Make the Dressing:** In a small bowl, whisk together rice vinegar, soy sauce, sesame oil, and grated fresh ginger until well combined.
3. **Combine:** Pour the dressing over the vegetables. Mix everything together until the dressing evenly coats all the vegetables.

Serving:

4. **Serve:** Serve the Sesame Ginger Slaw immediately, or let it chill in the refrigerator for a bit to allow the flavors to meld. Enjoy this crunchy and flavorful slaw as a side dish or topping.

TROPICAL AVOCADO SALAD

Servings: 4
Prep Time: 10 minutes
Total Ingredients: 8

Nutrition Facts (per serving):
Calories: 150 | Fat: 10g | Carbohydrates: 15g | Protein: 2g | Sodium: 50mg | Sugar: 10g

Ingredients:

- » 2 ripe mangoes, peeled and diced
- » 2 ripe avocados, peeled and diced
- » 1/4 cup red onion, finely chopped
- » 1/4 cup fresh cilantro, chopped
- » 1/4 cup fresh mint leaves, chopped
- » 2 tablespoons lime juice
- » 1 tablespoon olive oil
- » Salt and pepper to taste

Preparation:

1. **Prepare the Ingredients:** Peel and dice the mangoes and avocados. Finely chop the red onion, fresh cilantro, and fresh mint leaves.
2. **Make the Dressing:** In a small bowl, mix ogether lime juice, olive oil, salt, and pepper.
3. **Combine and Serve:** In a large bowl, gently toss the mango, avocado, red onion, cilantro, and mint with the dressing. Serve immediately, or refrigerate for 10 minutes before serving to let the flavors meld. Enjoy this vibrant and refreshing Tropical Avocado Salad.

CRUNCHY PEANUT AND RED CABBAGE SALAD

Servings: 4
Prep Time: 10 minutes
Total Ingredients: 8

Nutrition Facts (per serving):
Calories: 180 | Fat: 12g | Carbohydrates: 14g | Protein: 5g | Sodium: 200mg | Sugar: 6g

Ingredients:

» 2 cups shredded red cabbage
» 1 carrot, grated
» 1/4 cup roasted peanuts, chopped
» 2 green onions, sliced
» 1 tablespoon soy sauce
» 1 tablespoon lime juice
» 1 tablespoon olive oil
» 1 teaspoon maple syrup

Preparation:

1. **Prepare the Vegetables:** Shred the red cabbage and grate the carrot. Slice the green onions.
2. **Make the Dressing:** In a small bowl, whisk together soy sauce, lime juice, olive oil, and maple syrup.
3. **Combine and Serve:** In a large bowl, combine the shredded cabbage, grated carrot, chopped peanuts, and sliced green onions. Drizzle the salad with the dressing and toss well. Serve right away for a crunchy and refreshing side dish.

NAPA CABBAGE SALAD WITH MISO DRESSING

Servings: 4
Prep Time: 10 minutes
Total Ingredients: 8

Nutrition Facts (per serving): Calories: 70 | Fat: 4g | Carbohydrates: 7g | Protein: 2g | Sodium: 300mg | Sugar: 3g

Ingredients:

» 4 cups napa cabbage, thinly sliced
» 1 carrot, julienned
» 2 green onions, sliced
» 1 tablespoon white miso paste
» 2 tablespoons rice vinegar
» 1 tablespoon soy sauce
» 1 teaspoon sesame oil
» 1 teaspoon honey

Preparation:

1. **Prepare the Vegetables:** Thinly slice the napa cabbage, julienne the carrot, and slice the green onions.
2. **Make the Dressing:** In a small bowl, whisk together miso paste, rice vinegar, soy sauce, sesame oil, and honey until smooth.

Serving:

3. **Combine and Serve:** In a large bowl, combine the napa cabbage, carrot, and green onions. Pour the miso dressing over the vegetables and toss to coat. Serve right away for a crisp and flavorful salad.

Recipes Wok Cookbook for Beginners

CRISPY SPRING ROLLS

Servings: 4
Prep Time: 15 minutes
Cook Time: 15 minutes
Total Ingredients: 8

Nutrition Facts (per serving):
Calories: 200 | Fat: 8g | Carbohydrates: 28g | Protein: 4g | Sodium: 350mg | Sugar: 2g

Ingredients:

»   1 cup shredded cabbage
»   1/2 cup shredded carrots
»   1/2 cup bean sprouts
»   1/4 cup chopped green onions
»   1 tablespoon soy sauce
»   1 teaspoon sesame oil
»   1 package spring roll wrappers
»   Vegetable oil for frying

Preparation:

1. **Prepare the Filling:** In a large bowl, mix together shredded cabbage, shredded carrots, bean sprouts, chopped green onions, soy sauce, and sesame oil. Mix well to combine.

Cooking:

2. **Assemble the Rolls:** Place a spring roll wrapper on a clean work surface. Spoon about 2 tablespoons of filling onto the center of the wrapper. Fold the bottom corner up over the filling, then fold in the sides snugly, and roll it up tightly. Continue this process with the remaining wrappers and filling.

3. **Fry the Rolls:** Warm vegetable oil in a wok over medium-high heat. Once the oil is ready, carefully place the spring rolls in batches, frying until they achieve a golden brown and crispy texture, approximately 2-3 minutes per side. Lift them out and place them on paper towels to drain.

Serving:

4. **Serve the Rolls:** Arrange the golden spring rolls on a serving dish and accompany them with your preferred dipping sauce, such as sweet chili or soy sauce.

SHRIMP TEMPURA

Servings: 4
Prep Time: 10 minutes
Cook Time: 10 minutes
Total Ingredients: 7

Nutrition Facts (per serving):
Calories: 250 | Fat: 10g | Carbohydrates: 20g | Protein: 18g | Sodium: 300mg | Sugar: 1g

Ingredients:
» 1 lb large shrimp, peeled and deveined
» 1 cup all-purpose flour
» 1 egg, lightly beaten
» 1 cup cold sparkling water
» 1/2 teaspoon baking powder
» Vegetable oil for frying
» Tempura dipping sauce (optional)

Preparation:
1. **Prepare the Shrimp:** Pat the shrimp dry with paper towels. This will help the batter adhere better.
2. **Make the Batter:** In a bowl, mix together the flour and baking powder. Add the beaten egg and cold sparkling water, stirring just until combined. The batter should be slightly lumpy.

Cooking:
3. **Heat the Oil:** Heat vegetable oil in a wok over medium-high heat until it reaches 350°F.
4. **Fry the Shrimp:** Dip each shrimp into the batter, letting any excess drip back into the bowl. Gently place the shrimp into the hot oil, frying until they turn golden and crispy, around 2-3 minutes. Remove them and place on paper towels to drain.

Serving:
5. **Serve the Tempura:** Arrange the shrimp tempura on a serving plate. Serve immediately with tempura dipping sauce or soy sauce on the side.

WOK-SEARED EDAMAME

Servings: 4
Prep Time: 5 minutes
Cook Time: 10 minutes
Total Ingredients: 5

Nutrition Facts (per serving):
Calories: 120 | Fat: 6g | Carbohydrates: 10g | Protein: 8g | Sodium: 200mg | Sugar: 1g

Ingredients:

» 2 cups edamame in pods
» 1 tablespoon sesame oil
» 2 cloves garlic, minced
» 1 teaspoon soy sauce
» Sea salt, to taste

Preparation:

1. **Prepare the Edamame:** Give the edamame a rinse under cold water, then pat them dry.
2. **Heat the Oil:** Heat sesame oil in a wok over medium-high heat until shimmering.

Cooking:

3. **Stir-Fry the Edamame:** Add the minced garlic to the wok and stir-fry for 30 seconds until aromatic. Add the edamame and soy sauce, stir-frying for 5-7 minutes until the edamame are soft and slightly charred.

Serving:

4. **Serve the Edamame:** Remove from heat and place the edamame on a serving bowl. Add sea salt and serve immediately as a tasty, healthy snack.

SESAME CHICKEN BITES

Servings: 4
Prep Time: 10 minutes
Cook Time: 15 minutes
Total Ingredients: 9

Nutrition Facts (per serving):
Calories: 300 | Fat: 15g | Carbohydrates: 20g | Protein: 22g | Sodium: 500mg | Sugar: 1g

Ingredients:

» 1 lb boneless, skinless chicken breasts, cut into small pieces
» 1/4 cup all-purpose flour
» 1/4 cup cornstarch
» 1 egg, lightly beaten
» 2 tablespoons sesame oil
» 1/4 cup soy sauce
» 2 tablespoons honey
» 1 tablespoon sesame seeds
» Vegetable oil for frying

Preparation:

1. **Prepare the Batter:** In a bowl, mix the flour, cornstarch, and a pinch of salt. Separately, beat the egg. Dip each chicken piece in the egg, then coat with the flour mixture.
2. **Prepare the Sauce:** In a small bowl, mix together the sesame oil, soy sauce, and honey. Let it rest.

Cooking:

3. **Fry the Chicken:** Heat vegetable oil in a wok over medium-high heat. Fry the chicken pieces in batches until golden brown and cooked through, for 5-7 minutes. Take out and drain on paper towels.
4. **Toss in Sauce:** Heat the prepared sauce in the wok over medium heat. Add the fried chicken pieces and toss to coat. Add sesame seeds on top.

Serving:

5. **Serve the Chicken Bites:** Transfer the sesame chicken bites to a serving plate. Serve right away with a side of steamed rice or a dipping sauce.

SPICY TOFU BITES

Servings: 4
Prep Time: 10 minutes
Cook Time: 15 minutes
Total Ingredients: 8

Nutrition Facts (per serving):
Calories: 220 | Fat: 12g | Carbohydrates: 10g | Protein: 18g | Sodium: 600mg | Sugar: 2g

Ingredients:

» 1 block firm tofu, cut into tiny cubes
» 2 tablespoons soy sauce
» 1 tablespoon sriracha or chili garlic sauce
» 1 tablespoon hoisin sauce
» 1 teaspoon sesame oil
» 2 cloves garlic, minced
» 1 tablespoon cornstarch
» 2 tablespoons vegetable oil

Preparation:

1. **Marinate the Tofu:** In a bowl, combine soy sauce, sriracha, hoisin sauce, sesame oil, and minced garlic. Add the tofu cubes and toss to coat. Let marinate for 10 minutes.
2. **Coat with Cornstarch:** Sprinkle the cornstarch over the marinated tofu and toss to coat evenly.

Cooking:

3. **Stir-Fry the Tofu:** Heat vegetable oil in a wok over medium-high heat. Put in the tofu cubes and stir-fry them until they become crusty and golden brown, approximately 5-7 minutes.

Serving:

4. **Serve the Tofu Bites:** Transfer the spicy tofu bites to a platter. Serve hot with a side of steamed vegetables or a dipping sauce of your choice. Enjoy!

MANGO STICKY RICE

Servings: 4
Prep Time: 10 minutes
Cook Time: 20 minutes
Total Ingredients: 6

Nutrition Facts (per serving):
Calories: 350 | Fat: 10g | Carbohydrates: 65g | Protein: 4g | Sodium: 100mg | Cholesterol: 0mg

Ingredients:

» 1 cup glutinous rice (also known as sticky rice)
» 1 1/4 cups coconut milk
» 1/4 cup sugar
» 1/2 teaspoon salt
» 2 ripe mangoes, peeled and sliced
» 1 tablespoon toasted sesame seeds (optional, for garnish)

Preparation:

1. **Cook the Sticky Rice:** Rinse the glutinous rice under cold water until the water is completely clear. Soak the rice in water for at least 30 minutes, then drain.
2. In a wok, add the soaked rice and 1 1/4 cups of water. Bring the mixture to a boil, then lower the heat, cover, and let it gently simmer for approximately 15 minutes or until the water is absorbed and the rice is tender.

Cooking:

3. **Prepare the Coconut Sauce:** In a small saucepan, mix the coconut milk, sugar, and salt. Heat on medium, stirring consistently, until the sugar dissolves. Do not let it boil. Remove from heat and let it cool slightly.
4. **Mix the Rice with the Sauce:** Once the rice is cooked, move it onto a large bowl. Gradually pour 3/4 of the coconut sauce over the rice, stirring gently to combine. Let the rice absorb the sauce for about 10 minutes.

Serving:

5. **Plate the Dish:** Arrange the sliced mangoes on plates. Scoop a portion of the sticky rice onto each plate next to the mango slices. Drizzle the remaining coconut sauce over the sticky rice. Add toasted sesame seeds as garnish, if desired.
6. **Enjoy:** Serve warm or at room temperature. Enjoy your Mango Sticky Rice as a delightful finish to your meal.

COCONUT MILK PUDDING

Servings: 4

Prep Time: 10 minutes

Cook Time: 15 minutes
(plus chilling time)

Total Ingredients: 7

Nutrition Facts (per serving):

Calories: 280 | Fat: 18g | Carbohydrates: 28g | Protein: 3g | Sodium: 60mg | Cholesterol: 0mg

Ingredients:

» 2 cups coconut milk
» 1/4 cup sugar
» 1/4 cup cornstarch
» 1/2 teaspoon vanilla extract
» Pinch of salt
» Fresh fruit or toasted coconut flakes (optional, for garnish)
» Mint leaves (optional, for garnish)

Preparation:

1. **Prepare Ingredients:** In a small bowl, mix the cornstarch with 1/4 cup of coconut milk until smooth to make a slurry. Measure out the sugar and salt. Set aside vanilla extract and optional garnishes.

Cooking:

2. **Heat the Coconut Milk:** In a wok, combine the remaining coconut milk, sugar, and salt. Heat over medium heat, stirring constantly until the sugar dissolves and the mixture begins to simmer.
3. **Thicken the Pudding:** Slowly incorporate the cornstarch slurry into the wok, maintaining constant stirring to avoid lumps. Continue to cook, stirring frequently, until the mixture thickens, for 5-7 minutes. It should coat the back of a spoon.
4. **Flavor the Pudding:** Remove the wok from heat and whisk in the vanilla extract.

Serving:

5. **Chill the Pudding:** Pour the pudding into individual serving dishes or ramekins. Let it cool slightly before covering with plastic wrap. Place in the fridge for at least 2 hours or until fully set.
6. **Garnish and Serve:** Before serving, garnish with fresh fruit, toasted coconut flakes, and mint leaves if desired. Serve chilled.

FRIED BANANA SPRING ROLLS

Servings: 4
Prep Time: 10 minutes
Cook Time: 10 minutes
Total Ingredients: 5

Nutrition Facts (per serving):
Calories: 250 | Fat: 8g | Carbohydrates: 40g | Protein: 3g | Sodium: 150mg | Sugar: 18g

Ingredients:

» 4 ripe bananas, cut in half lengthwise
» 8 spring roll wrappers
» 1/4 cup honey
» 1/4 cup vegetable oil
» Powdered sugar (optional, for dusting)

Preparation:

1. **Prepare the Spring Rolls:** Place a banana half on a spring roll wrapper. Fold the sides inward over the banana, then roll it up tightly. Dab a bit of water along the edges to seal. Do this with the remaining bananas and wrappers.

Cooking:

2. **Fry the Spring Rolls:** Set a wok over medium-high heat and add the vegetable oil. Deep-fry the spring rolls in batches for 2-3 minutes on each side, until golden brown. Remove and let dry on paper towels.

Serving:

3. **Serve the Dish:** Arrange the fried banana spring rolls on a serving plate. Drizzle with honey and dust with powdered sugar if desired. Serve warm with a scoop of vanilla ice cream for an extra treat.

SWEET RED BEAN PANCAKES

Servings: 4
Prep Time: 10 minutes
Cook Time: 15 minutes
Total Ingredients: 7

Nutrition Facts (per serving):
Calories: 180 | Fat: 3g | Carbohydrates: 35g | Protein: 5g | Sodium: 200mg | Sugar: 12g

Ingredients:

» 1 cup all-purpose flour
» 1/2 cup milk
» 1 egg
» 2 tablespoons sugar
» 1 teaspoon baking powder
» 1/4 teaspoon salt
» 1/2 cup sweet red bean paste (anko)

Preparation:

1. **Prepare the Batter:** In a bowl, mix together the flour, milk, egg, sugar, baking powder, and salt until smooth.

Cooking:

2. **Cook the Pancakes:** Set a nonstick wok over medium-high heat. To make a pancake, scoop 1/4 cup of batter into the wok. Once surface bubbles appear, turn and continue to cook until golden brown. Do it again with the rest of the batter.
3. **Fill the Pancakes:** Spread 2 tablespoons of sweet red bean paste on one pancake, then top with another pancake to form a sandwich.

Serving:

4. **Serve the Pancakes:** Enjoy the delicious blend of sweet red bean filling and fluffy pancakes served warm.

CARAMELIZED PINEAPPLE RINGS

Servings: 4
Prep Time: 5 minutes
Cook Time: 10 minutes
Total Ingredients: 5

Nutrition Facts (per serving):
Calories: 180 | Fat: 0g | Carbohydrates: 45g | Protein: 1g | Sodium: 10mg | Cholesterol: 0mg

Ingredients:

» 1 fresh pineapple, peeled, cored, and cut into 1/2-inch rings
» 1/2 cup brown sugar
» 1/4 cup coconut milk
» 2 tablespoons unsalted butter
» 1 teaspoon vanilla extract

Preparation:

1. **Prepare the Pineapple:** Peel, core, and slice the pineapple into 1/2-inch thick rings.

Cooking:

2. **Heat the Wok:** Preheat the wok over medium heat. Add the butter and let it melt.
3. **Caramelize the Sugar:** Add the brown sugar to the melted butter in the wok. Stir continuously until the sugar melts and turns into a caramel sauce, for 2-3 minutes.
4. **Add the Pineapple:** Place the pineapple rings into the caramel sauce. Cook for 2-3 minutes on each side, or until the pineapple is tender and golden brown.
5. **Finish the Sauce:** Pour in the coconut milk and vanilla extract. Stir to combine and let it simmer for another 2 minutes. The sauce should thicken and coat the pineapple rings.

Serving:

6. **Serve the Pineapple:** Place the caramelized pineapple rings onto a platter. Pour any remaining sauce over the top.
7. **Optional Garnishes:** Garnish with a sprinkle of toasted coconut flakes or a scoop of vanilla ice cream for an extra treat.

MEASUREMENT CONVERSION CHART

COOKING MEASUREMENT CHART

WEIGHT

IMPERIAL	METRIC
1/2 oz	15 g
1 oz	29 g
2 oz	57 g
3 oz	85 g
4 oz	113 g
5 oz	141 g
6 oz	170 g
8 oz	227 g
10 oz	283 g
12 oz	340 g
13 oz	369 g
14 oz	397 g
15 oz	425 g
1 lb	453 g

MEASUREMENT

CUP	ONCES	MILLILITERS	TABLESPOONS
8 cup	64 oz	1895 ml	128
6 cup	48 oz	1420 ml	96
5 cup	40 oz	1180 ml	80
4 cup	32 oz	960 ml	64
2 cup	16 oz	480 ml	32
1 cup	8 oz	240 ml	16
3/4 cup	6 oz	177 ml	12
2/3 cup	5 oz	158 ml	11
1/2 cup	4 oz	118 ml	8
3/8 cup	3 oz	90 ml	6
1/3 cup	2.5 oz	79 ml	5.5
1/4 cup	2 oz	59 ml	4
1/8 cup	1 oz	30 ml	3
1/16 cup	1/2 oz	15 ml	1

TEMPERATURE

FARENHEIT	CELSIUS
100 °F	37 °C
150 °F	65 °C
200 °F	93 °C
250 °F	121 °C
300 °F	150 °C
325 °F	160 °C
350 °F	180 °C
375 °F	190 °C
400 °F	200 °C
425 °F	220 °C
450 °F	230 °C
500 °F	260 °C
525 °F	274 °C
550 °F	288 °C

Recipes Wok Cookbook for Beginners

GRAB YOUR BONUS!

As a thank you for purchasing this book, we're offering you 5 exclusive bonuses:

1. **eBook "Free Color Edition"**: Enjoy a vibrant, color edition of this cookbook with your purchase.
2. **eBook "Party-Perfect Wok Recipes"**: Impress your guests with spectacular wok dishes perfect for entertaining.
3. **eBook "Global Wok Adventures"**: Expand your culinary horizons with wok recipes from around the world.
4. **eBook "Skillet Sensations"**: Complement your wok cooking with these additional skillet recipes.
5. **eBook "Mastering Advanced Techniques"**: Take your skills to the next level with advanced recipes and techniques.

To claim your bonuses, please email us at
info@edhousemedia.com
with "*Wok Cookbook Bonus*" in the subject line.

CONCLUSION

Many congratulations on finishing your journey through "Wok Cookbook for Beginners." You've started down the exciting and tasty path of wok cooking, investigating a range of techniques, ingredients, and dishes that highlight the remarkable adaptability of this age-old cooking style.

You can easily prepare tasty meals now, from stir-frying to fast, healthy dinners. A kitchen's essential equipment, the wok has the ability to cook food quickly while preserving its tastes or textures. You'll find great use for the skills you've gained, whether you're cooking for a crowd or just yourself.

We've emphasized in this cookbook the importance of flavor harmony and balance, the use of easily available, fresh ingredients, and the excitement of trying new recipes.

As you go on learning about wok cooking, remember that practice and experimentation are essential. Try different dishes, change the ingredients, and personalize each one.

Thank you for choosing this cookbook. I hope it has sparked a passion for wok cooking and added excitement to your kitchen.

Made in the USA
Monee, IL
18 December 2024

74375569R00061